SHEPHERD'S NOTES

Shepherd's Notes Titles Available

SHEPHERD'S NOTES COMMENTARY SERIES

Old Testament

0-80549-028-0	Genesis	0-80549-341-7	Psalms 101-150
0-80549-056-6	Exodus	0-80549-016-7	Proverbs
0-80549-069-8	Leviticus & Numbers	0-80549-059-0	Ecclesiastes, Song of
0-80549-027-2	Deuteronomy		Solomon
0-80549-058-2	Joshua & Judges	0-80549-197-X	Isaiah
0-80549-057-4	Ruth & Esther	0-80549-070-1	Jeremiah-
0-80549-063-9	1 & 2 Samuel		Lamentations
0-80549-007-8	1 & 2 Kings	0-80549-078-7	Ezekiel
0-80549-064-7	1 & 2 Chronicles	0-80549-015-9	Daniel
0-80549-194-5	Ezra, Nehemiah	0-80549-326-3	Hosea-Obadiah
0-80549-006-X	Job	0-80549-334-4	Jonah-Zephaniah
0-80549-339-5	Psalms 1-50	0-80549-065-5	Haggai-Malachi
0-80549-340-9	Psalms 51-100		

New Testament

1-55819-688-9	Matthew	1-55819-689-7	Philippians,
0-80549-071-X	Mark		Colossians, &
0-80549-004-3	Luke		Philemon
1-55819-693-5	John	0-80549-000-0	1 & 2 Thessalonians
1-55819-691-9	Acts	1-55819-692-7	1 & 2 Timothy, Titus
0-80549-005-1	Romans	0-80549-336-0	Hebrews
0-80549-325-5	1 Corinthians	0-80549-018-3	James
0-80549-335-2	2 Corinthians	0-80549-019-1	1 & 2 Peter & Jude
1-55819-690-0	Galatians	0-80549-214-3	1, 2 & 3 John
0-80549-327-1	Ephesians	0-80549-017-5	Revelation

SHEPHERD'S NOTES CHRISTIAN CLASSICS

0-80549-347-6	Mere Christianity-C.S.Lewis	0-80549-394-8	Miracles-C.S.Lewis
0-80549-353-0	The Problem of Pain/ A Grief Observed-C.S.Lewis	0-80549-196-1	Lectures to My Students-Charles Haddon Spurgeon
0-80549-199-6	The Confessions-Augustine	0-80549-220-8	The Writings of Justin Martyr
0-80549-200-3	Calvin's Institutes	0-80549-345-X	The City of God

SHEPHERD'S NOTES-BIBLE SUMMARY SERIES

0-80549-377-8	Old Testament	0-80549-385-9	Life & Letters of Paul
0-80549-378-6	New Testament	0-80549-376-X	Manners & Customs of Bible Times
0-80549-384-0	Life & Teachings of Jesus	0-80549-380-8	Basic Christian Beliefs

SHEPHERD'S NOTES

When you need a guide through the Scriptures

James

Nashville, Tennessee

Shepherd's Notes—*James*
© 1998
by Broadman & Holman Publishers
Nashville, Tennessee
All rights reserved
Printed in the United States of America

Dewey Decimal Classification: 227.9
Subject Heading: BIBLE N.T. JAMES
Library of Congress Card Catalog Number: 98–15308

ISBN-10: 0-8054-9018-3
ISBN-13: 978-0-8054-9018-3

Library of Congress Cataloging-in-Publication Data
James / Dana Gould, editor
    p. cm. — (Shepherd's notes)
    Includes bibliographical references.
    ISBN 0–8054–9018–3
    1. Bible. N.T. James—Study and teaching. I. Gould, Dana. 1951– .
II. Series.
BS2785.5.J35 1998
227'.91'007—dc21

98–15308
CIP

7 8 9 10 11   09 08 07 06

CONTENTS

Dear Reader:

Shepherd's Notes are designed to give you a quick, step-by-step overview of every book of the Bible. They are not meant to be substitutes for the biblical text; rather, they are study guides intended to help you explore the wisdom of Scripture in personal or group study and to apply that wisdom successfully in your own life.

Shepherd's Notes guide you through the main themes of each book of the Bible and illuminate fascinating details through appropriate commentary and reference notes. Historical and cultural background information brings the Bible into sharper focus.

Six different icons, used throughout the series, call your attention to historical-cultural information, Old Testament and New Testament references, word pictures, unit summaries, and personal application for everyday life.

Whether you are a novice or a veteran at Bible study, I believe you will find *Shepherd's Notes* a resource that will take you to a new level in your mining and applying the riches of Scripture.

In Him,

David R. Shepherd
Editor-in-Chief

DESIGNED FOR THE BUSY USER

Shepherd's Notes for James is designed to provide an easy-to-use tool for getting a quick handle on this Bible book's important features, and for gaining an understanding of the message of James. Information available in more difficult-to-use reference works has been incorporated into the *Shepherd's Notes* format. This brings you the benefits of many more advanced and expensive works packed into one small volume.

Shepherd's Notes are for laymen, pastors, teachers, small-group leaders and participants, as well as the classroom student. Enrich your personal study or quiet time. Shorten your class or small-group preparation time as you gain valuable insights into the truths of God's Word that you can pass along to your students or group members.

DESIGNED FOR QUICK ACCESS

Those with time constraints will especially appreciate the timesaving features built into the *Shepherd's Notes*. All features are intended to aid a quick and concise encounter with the heart of the message.

Concise Commentary. James is one of the most practical books in the Bible. Short sections provide quick "snapshots" of passages, highlighting important points and other information.

Outlined Text. A comprehensive outline covers the entire text of James. This is a valuable feature for following the narrative's flow, allowing for a quick, easy way to locate a particular passage.

Shepherd's Notes. These summary statements appear at the close of every key section of the narrative. While functioning in part as a quick summary, they also deliver the essence of the message presented in the sections they cover.

Icons. Various icons in the margin highlight recurring themes in James, aiding in selective searching or tracing of those themes.

Sidebars and Charts. These specially selected features provide additional background information to your study or preparation. These include definitions as well as cultural, historical, and biblical insights.

Maps. These are placed at appropriate places in the book to aid your understanding and study of a text or passage.

Questions to Guide Your Study. These thought-provoking questions and discussion starters are designed to encourage interaction with the truth and principles of God's Word.

In addition to the above features, study aids have been included at the back of the book for those readers who require or desire more information and resources for working through James. A list of reference sources used for this volume is provided which offers many works that allow the reader to extend the scope of his or her study of this letter.

DESIGNED TO WORK FOR YOU

Personal Study. Using the *Shepherd's Notes* with a passage of Scripture can enlighten your study and take it to a new level. At your fingertips is information that would require searching several volumes to find. In addition, many points of application occur throughout the volume, contributing to personal growth.

Teaching. Outlines frame the text of James and provide a logical presentation of the message. *Shepherd's Notes* icons provide summary statements for presenting the essence of key points and events. Personal Application icons point out personal application of the message of James, and Historical Context icons indicate where background information is supplied.

Group Study. Shepherd's Notes can be an excellent companion volume to use for gaining a quick but accurate understanding of the message of a Bible book. Each group member can benefit by having his or her own copy. The *Note's* format accommodates the study of or the tracing of the themes throughout James. Leaders may use its flexible features to prepare for group sessions, or use during group sessions. Questions to Guide Your Study can spark discussion of the key points and truths of James.

LIST OF MARGIN ICONS USED IN JAMES

Shepherd's Notes. Placed at the end of each section, a capsule statement provides the reader with the essence of the message of that section.

Old Testament Reference. To indicate a prophecy fulfillment and its discussion in the text.

New Testament Reference. Used when the writer refers to New Testament passages that are related to or have a bearing on the passage's understanding or interpretation.

Historical Background. Historical Context. To indicate historical information—historical, biographical, cultural—and provide insight on the understanding or interpretation of a passage.

Personal Application. Used when the text provides a personal or universal application of truth.

Word Picture. Indicates that the meaning of a specific word or phrase is illustrated so as to shed light on it.

INTRODUCTION

The letter of James belongs to the section of the New Testament usually described as the General Epistles. The letter is one of exhortation for practical Christianity. The author states principles of conduct and then frequently provides poignant illustrations. The author's concerns are clearly more practical and less abstract than those of any other New Testament writer. No other New Testament book has received the level of criticism encountered by this epistle.

JAMES IN A "NUTSHELL"	
Purpose:	To call individuals and the church to full commitment to God and to concern for one another
Major Doctrine:	Genuine faith that is evidenced by good works
Key Passage:	"Be doers of the word, and not merely hearers who deceive themselves" (1:22, NRSV)
Other Key Doctrines:	Prayer; judgment; grace; intercession

THE MAIN THEME OF JAMES

James's letter makes a unique contribution in the New Testament with its strong ethical emphasis. Its ethical teaching is scattered throughout his writing. James clearly taught that a faith that lacks works is empty, vain, and useless. James's frequent use of the imperative mood (in the Greek language which he used to write the letter) indicates his passionate feeling about the issues he faced. His fiery words resemble those of an Old Testament prophet. He shared ethical commands that touched upon both personal morality and social justice.

Church councils meeting at Rome (A.D. 382) and Carthage (A.D. 397) accepted the book of James as Scripture. This acceptance gave support to the view that James, the Lord's brother, was the author.

AUTHOR

The book of James came slowly into widespread circulation in the early church. Many factors contributed to this. Its brevity and practical nature made it seem of small significance in comparison to a book like Romans. Christians in the early church also disagreed concerning the identity of James, the author of the letter. Those who identified the name with the Lord's brother tended to view the letter as genuine Scripture. Those who rejected the link between James and Jesus tended to ignore the letter.

Bible students debate the precise meaning of "the Lord's brother" (Gal. 1:19). Possibilities are the literal brother or stepbrother, a cousin, or intimate friend or associate. The literal meaning is preferred.

Paul, seeking out Peter in Jerusalem after his conversion, reported "I saw none of the other apostles—only James, the Lord's brother" (Gal. 1:19). In time, James assumed the leadership of the Jerusalem church, originally held by Peter. Evidently, such was achieved not through a power struggle but by James's constancy with the church while Peter and other apostles traveled.

In a Jerusalem conference called regarding Paul's Gentile mission, James presided as spokesman for the Jerusalem church (Acts 15). James perceived his calling as to the "circumcised," that is, the Jews (Gal. 2:9), and is portrayed as loyal to Jewish tradition. He was, however, unwilling to make the law normative for all people who responded to God's new action in Christ.

The death of James reportedly was at the order of priestly authorities in Jerusalem and was either by stoning (according to Flavius Josephus, first-century historian of the Jews) or by being cast down from the Temple tower (after Hegesippus, early Christian writer, quoted by the third-century historian Eusebius). These accounts of James's death (about A.D. 66), are not confirmed in the New Testament.

The text of James provides little information about the author other than his name, but its mention provides an important clue to his identity. Few persons with the name of James could succeed in identifying themselves merely by their first name. The writer must have been an important James.

Other features of the letter also confirm the likelihood of identifying the author with Jesus' brother. James 1:22 and 5:12 contain echoes of Jesus' teaching in Matt. 7:20–24 and 5:34–37, respectively. The brother of the Lord could have heard this teaching. While it is not possible to prove beyond a shadow of a doubt that the Lord's brother is the author of this letter, he is the most likely candidate from among the men named James mentioned in the New Testament.

PURPOSE FOR WRITING

The letter is pastoral in purpose, and we see several purposes that James targets within its pages:

- It encourages those besieged by trials.
- It rebukes the prejudiced.
- It condemns an idle faith that will not work.
- It instructs with regard to the tongue.
- It explains the nature of pure religion.
- It counsels concerning the ministries to the sick.
- It shows concern for evangelism.

"In a book written in 1915, the great Greek scholar A. T. Robertson chose for his title *Practical and Social Aspects of Christianity*. That title appropriately picks up the theme of this particularly powerful epistle" (taken from Foy Valentine, *Hebrews, James, 1 & 2 Peter*, Layman's Bible Book Commentary [Nashville: Broadman & Holman Publishers, 1981], 67).

DATE OF WRITING

Many scholars feel that the book of James is one of the earlier New Testament writings. Three features suggest an early date:

James, the Lord's brother, was martyred in A.D. 62. If he was the author of the letter, the letter was written before A.D. 62.

1. James describes a large gap between the rich and the poor (5:1–6). When the war against Rome broke out in A.D. 66, the rich suffered great losses, and conflict between the rich and poor ceased. The impact of this observation pushes the writing to an earlier time rather than later.

2. The church organization mentioned in James seems undeveloped as seen in the mention only of elders as church leaders (5:14).

3. Christians were fervently expecting the return of Christ (5:7–9). Such fervor would be more true of the initial generations of Christians. All of these features support the acceptance of an earlier date for the writing of James.

AUDIENCE

The letter lacks an address to a specific church. The address of the letter is to "the twelve tribes scattered among the nations" (1:1). The twelve tribes were social and political groups in Israel claiming descent from one of the twelve sons of Jacob. These tribes were Reuben, Simeon, Levi, Judah, Issachar, Zebulun, Joseph, Ephraim, Manasseh, Benjamin, Dan, and Naphtali. Each tribe had its own history within its allotment of land.

The tribes became scattered across many nations. The dispersion, or *diaspora*, refers to this scattering of the tribes. The dispersion of the tribes most likely began at the time of the Assyrian captivity and took place over a span of several centuries. The result of the *diaspora* was that by New Testament times, as many Jews lived outside of Palestine as lived within the land. In almost every city Paul visited in his missionary journeys, he found a Jewish synagogue. The *diaspora* helped pave the way for the gospel.

This suggests that the readers were Jewish Christians who lived outside of Palestine. Several features confirm the truth of this suggestion:

1. The term for "meeting" (2:2) is the Greek word for "synagogue." The word does not suggest that the readers met in a Jewish synagogue, but it indicates that Jewish Christians used this name to describe their place of meeting.
2. The phrase "scattered among the nations" (1:1) reflects a single Greek word that referred to Jews who lived out of their homeland.

These facts suggest that the Lord's brother directed a message to Jewish believers who had left their native country of Palestine.

LITERARY FEATURES IN JAMES

Literary Form

James's writing is similar to Old Testament wisdom literature in Proverbs and Psalms. Both James and Old Testament wisdom literature treat such subjects as the tongue, the dangers of wealth, and the need for self-control. The content of the letter moves quickly from one subject to another. Some scholars have also pointed out a similarity with synagogue homilies or sermons.

James's writing reflects a vivid imagination. We can see his use of various figures of speech in his comparison of the wavering person to "a wave of the sea, blown and tossed by the wind" (1:6). He was also a close observer of nature. We can see this from his description of the effects of the sun's heat (1:11), horticulture (3:12), and rainfall (5:7, 18).

James used several basic literary forms to deliver his letter:

1. The entire book is framed in the *epistolary*, or letter, form.
2. He uses the *diatribe*, a teaching device for exhorting moral reform in his readers.
3. He also uses *parenesis*, traditional moral instruction in the form of loose sets of proverbs.

Key Words

"These connecting words are designed for didactic purposes, to render the teaching easy to memorize" (Nigel Turner, *Grammar of the Greek New Testament*, vol. IV [Edinburgh: T. & T. Clark, 1976]), 116.)

Throughout James we see recurring connecting or "chain" words that form threads of the key themes in the letter. These words include temptation, patience, perfection, lacking, asking, wavering, lust, sin, slowness, wrath, word, hearer, beholding, and doer.

Literary Devices

James employed several literary devices throughout his writing that are effective tools for providing emphasis, gaining the reader's attention, and communicating spiritual truth. The following are a few of his most-used devices.

Short Questions and Answers. Regularly through-out these chapters James poses short, staccato-like questions that he then follows with an answer. For example:

- "Who is wise and understanding among you? Let him show it" (3:13).
- "What is your life? You are a mist that appears for a little while" (4:14).
- "Is any one of you in trouble? He should pray" (5:13).

Rhetorical Questions. James is fond of this kind of question, for which he does not provide a direct answer. For example:

- "Has not God chosen those who are poor?" (2:5).
- "What good is it?" (2:14).
- "Can a fig tree bear olives?" (3:12).

Questions of Irony. Irony is expression of a thought that naturally conveys its opposite. Irony is often connected with serious words and concepts. For example:

- "If a man claims to have faith but has no deeds" (2:14).
- "You rich people, weep and wail" (5:1).

JAMES AND THE GOSPELS

James echoes many of the themes found in the four Gospels. In his letter are many parallels to the teachings of Jesus, including several striking passages from the Sermon on the Mount (Matt. 5–7). The themes he did not include are somewhat surprising, such as the person and work of Jesus Christ, the work of the Holy Spirit, the practice of baptism and the Lord's Supper, and the gifts of the church and its nature as a spiritual body.

JAMES AND THE WRITINGS OF PAUL

The apparent contradiction between James and Paul regarding faith and works is just that—apparent. James was not struggling against Judaizing Christianity, which sought to require circumcision in addition to faith in Christ. He was not trying to "correct" Paul at key points (e.g., Rom. 3:20; Gal. 2:16). He was concerned with the consistency of genuine faith as evidenced by its results, that faith should be active, not a mere profession covering a life of sin.

JAMES AND THEOLOGY

Doctrines in the Book of James

Some students of James suggest that the book lacks doctrinal emphases. It is true that James assumed some doctrinal similarity between himself and his readers and did not elaborate on all his beliefs. He does affirm the unity of God (2:19; 4:12) together with an emphasis on divine goodness (1:17), graciousness (4:6–8), and judgment (2:13). He emphasizes strongly the return of Christ (5:7–11). In 1:12–15 he presents an analysis of temptation and sin, suggesting that human desire was the source of sin. Much of the content of James represents an effort to call individuals and the church back to full commitment to God and to concern for one another.

"Every good and every perfect gift is from above, and cometh down from the Father of lights, with whom is no variableness, neither shadow of turning" (James 1:17, KJV).

End Times. Trials and testings are presented in view of the revelation of the end-time rule of God. It is this prospect over which believers are called to rejoice and persevere. Judgment is certain, especially upon the rich, who have oppressed others.

Faith and Deeds. Deeds demonstrate the genuineness of one's faith. The way believers live must correspond to the claims they make for their faith. James harshly attacks contradictions between faith and life. Faith is primary in his letter—but only faith which is true, active, consistent, and genuine.

Ethical Teachings. James showed a concern for reforming Christian behavior. He effectively developed several ethical topics: speech, trials, wealth, and mercy. His contrast between the rich and poor is very obvious. Like the Old Testament prophets, James attacked wealthy believers who contradicted the truth of their faith by withholding the acts of love and mercy required of them.

Law. James's concept of the law draws upon Lev. 19:18, which sums up the whole law in the command to love God and neighbor. This law is integral to faith, leading to the mercy and love God requires of those who trust Him.

"Thou shalt not avenge, nor bear any grudge against the children of thy people, but thou shalt love they neighbor as thyself: I am the Lord" (Lev. 19:18, KJV).

Wisdom. Wisdom is the gift of God. By wisdom, believers translated their present trials into opportunities to trust in and do the will of God. The necessity of wisdom deepens as James comes closer to the description of true faith that contrasts with the foolishness of those who imagine that living faith does not express itself in obedience.

Human Nature. James pointed out that conflicts between faith and the temptation to sin find their source within fallen human nature. Human beings are created in and possess the qualities of the image of God, but they are also their own sources of evil desire.

Church. James does not supply direct teaching on the nature of the church but presupposes it. The local church possessed a plurality of elders upon whom the sick were to call for prayer, but

9

James gave no indication of the nature of their authority.

God. God the Creator receives praise throughout the body of James's letter. That He created the universe and sustains it is summed up by the title "Father of lights." God is generous and merciful, but He is also the Judge and Lawgiver. The doctrine of God is presupposed in James rather than extensively developed.

In 2:1 James refers to Christ as "the Lord of glory" (KJV).

Christ. James made it clear that Jesus Christ is the Lord whom he served. Christ shares this title with God (the Father). He is also called "glorious," fully sharing the glory that belongs to God alone. With these titles, Christ is identified with God.

Theological Significance of the Book of James

James reminds us in a forthright way that faith involves doing. It is not enough to be hearers of the word; we must be doers as well. We cannot just say we are believers; we must show it in our lives. This must be evident in the way we control our tongues and the way we relate to others. The rich must share with the poor. The Christian community must live out its faith by demonstrating love and a working faith to those inside and outside the body of Christ.

THE RELEVANCE OF JAMES FOR BELIEVERS TODAY

James encouraged his readers in the trials and tribulations of life and challenged them to engage in right living. His letter remains of lasting value and consequence to the Christian confronted by an increasingly secular world. The theme and mandate of James is that Christ ought to make a difference in a believer's life. That mandate is just as relevant today as it was when James addressed his original readers.

BASIC OUTLINE FOR JAMES
  I. Greeting (1:1)
 II. How to Face Trials (1:2–18)
III. A Correct Response to God's Word
     (1:19–27)
 IV. The Avoidance of Partiality (2:1–13)
  V. The Production of Works of Mercy
     (2:14–26)
 VI. The Practice of Personal Discipline (3:1–18)
VII. The Avoidance of Worldliness (4:1–17)
VIII.The Demonstration of Justice (5:1–6)
 IX. The Practice of Endurance (5:7–12)
  X. The Proper Use of Prayer (5:13–18)
 XI. The Reclamation of Straying Christians
     (5:19–20)

QUESTIONS TO GUIDE YOUR STUDY
 1. What is the main theme of James's letter?
 2. Who were James's readers? What makes
    his message relevant to today's readers?
 3. What do we know about the author of
    this letter?
 4. What is the apparent contradiction some
    see between what James taught and the
    writings of the apostle Paul?

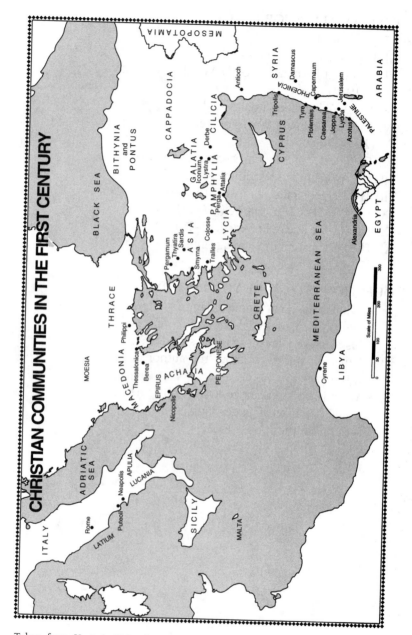

Taken from Kurt A. Richardson, *James*, vol. 36, New American Commentary (Nashville, Tenn. Broadman & Holman Publishers), 20.

In this first chapter, James began by showing the attitude of a compassionate pastor shepherding his flock through trials. Then he wrote with the fire of an Old Testament prophet as he warned against sinful activities and attitudes and called for changed behavior. In the midst of times of trial, believers may take comfort in the certainty of God's goodness and draw strength from God's Word.

The Diaspora

The diaspora was the scattering of the Jews from the land of Palestine into other parts of the world. The term *dispersion* is often used to describe this process.

GREETINGS (1:1)

From the Author. The writer of this letter identified himself only as "James, a servant of God and of the Lord Jesus Christ." It is significant that James chose not to mention his relationship to Jesus. His statement that he is a servant of Jesus indicates his humility. He did not allow his special relationship to Jesus to imply a unique authority for his teaching.

(See "Introduction" for a discussion of the authorship of the book of James.)

To His Readers. James's readers were the "twelve tribes scattered among the nations." The "twelve tribes" was a term commonly used to describe the nation Israel, God's chosen people as a whole. Comparing this passage with the apostle Paul's view of the church (Eph. 2 and Rom. 11), we see that the church does not displace Israel as God's beloved people, but that it does participate in a new covenant that will ultimately be the fulfillment of God's original covenant with Abraham and Moses.

HOW TO FACE TRIALS (1:2–8)

This first section of James presents trials in both their positive and negative aspects. Trials are to be viewed as a reason for rejoicing since vital faith is required by God. Trials serve as faith's stimulus. The guiding principle of this entire first chapter is the right understanding of wisdom. A right understanding refers to a life that puts faith and action together.

Trials Lead to Maturity (vv. 2–4)

The first readers of this letter, having been scattered and living outside Palestine, are likely experiencing serious adversity. This adversity could have taken many forms, such as loneliness, grief, suffering, hardship, rejection, frustration, homesickness, social isolation, language barriers, and culture shock. Actual persecution might have already begun.

James began with encouragement. He exhorted his readers to "consider it pure joy . . . whenever you face trials" (v. 2). James's reference to trials had in mind specific sufferings his readers were enduring. Because all things, including one's trials, work together for good for those who love God and are called according to His purpose, Christians are not to thrash about in frustration as troubles come.

Believers face many different kinds of trials. These trials come from different sources—opponents, doubts, fears, and tribulation.

Many kinds

The Greek word for this phrase can also mean multifaceted or multicolored.

The Greek word behind the English word for "face" is an interesting compound word made up of the preposition "around" and the verb "to fall." It can be rendered "to fall in with or among," or "to come across, encounter." One who "falls into" a trial normally does not have the option of taking or leaving it. These are unwanted and unwelcomed experiences. In a sense, one is "surrounded" without avenues for escape. When encountered, trials are to be endured and worked through. For the believer, this is a necessary process for maturing in the faith.

For the believer, trials are not accidents or purposeless. In verses 3–4 James provides his readers with the purpose for trials:

- the testing of the believer's faith produces perseverance;
- perseverance produces spiritual maturity.

James tells us that the testing of the believer's faith "develops" perseverance, and that this perseverance "works" toward maturity.

Purpose in the Testing of the Believer's Faith

PROCESS	PROCESS	FINAL RESULT
Testing Develops	Perseverance Develops	Maturity

In verse 4 James revealed the grand goal of the testing of the believer's faith: "that you may be mature and complete, not lacking anything."

"So that you may be mature and complete, not lacking anything" (v. 4) is not James's advice for Christians to achieve an obviously impossible sinless perfection. It is, rather, a powerful reminder that God's people must not surrender to trouble. On the contrary, believers must endure trials faithfully and stand steady through the storms of life. When such steadfastness has "its full effect" (NRSV), then God's faithful people will be "mature, not lacking anything" (Foy Valentine, *Hebrews, James, 1 & 2 Peter*, Layman's Bible Book Commentary,

Testing of faith

The word for "testing" is the word meaning "tested and approved." The purpose of the testing is not to find a person lacking, but to approve the genuineness of one's faith, or the genuine element of one's faith. The result of the trial is that true faith is proven to be authentic. The Greeks used this word to describe the testing of metals. "Your faith like gold stands the test of fire and is approved as standard" (A. T. Robertson, *Word Pictures in the New Testament*, vol. 6, "General Epistles and Revelation of John," 12).

vol. 23 [Nashville: Broadman & Holman Publishers, 1981], 70).

N

■ *James urged his readers to look at trials from*
■ *God's point of view. The trial itself is not an*
■ *occasion of joy, but it could promote joy by*
■ *becoming an occasion for producing stamina*
■ *in the life of a believer.*

Seeking Wisdom Through Prayer (vv. 5–8)

James's letter might appropriately be titled "The Wisdom of James." A quick reading of the entire letter reveals the author's deep concern for wisdom. At a very early point in the letter, he introduces this topic of special importance.

Wisdom is attainment of worthy ends by the use of worthy means. As used by James, wisdom is right understanding, moral discernment, spiritual insight, responsible words, and worthy deeds. *Wisdom* is not a word which occurs very often in our modern-day newspapers, TV, radio, at the cafeteria, or on the internet.

Praying for Wisdom (v. 5). James encouraged his readers, "If any of you lacks wisdom, he should ask God, who gives generously to all without finding fault" (v. 5). Facts may be gathered by inquiring minds, and scientific data can be accumulated and processed by experts in their fields, but wisdom is the special provision of God. To pray to God for wisdom is to recognize the fact that He knows all, and to acknowledge His providence. God delights in freely giving His great gift of wisdom, without finding fault with those who ask Him.

The wisdom that Christians are to pray for has deep roots in the soil of faith. James taught that there is a close connection between faith, prayer, and wisdom. The Christian who asks for wisdom asks in faith; asking in faith requires divine wisdom. To ask for this wisdom is wise in itself. Growth in wisdom is to understand that everything of faith is from God. Such wisdom sought through prayer is a fundamental characteristic of the believer's life in Christ.

Asking with Doubting (vv. 6–7). In verse 6, however, James warned his readers that those who ask must believe and not doubt that they will receive wisdom from God. James then used simile, a picture from nature, to illustrate the kind of person who doubts. That person is "like a wave of the sea, blown and tossed by the wind." It is the picture of a rudderless ship on the restless, swaying surface of the sea that is being whipped into whitecaps by the buffeting winds. It is a picture of an unstable vessel going nowhere fast. The believer who doubts his or her relationship with God exposes the instability of faith, and will not receive wisdom from God.

The word James used for "wave" is one that refers to a dashing or surging wave in contrast to successive waves (see A. T. Robertson, *Word Pictures in the New Testament*, vol. 6, "General Epistles and Revelation of John," 14).

Being Double-Minded (v. 8). To pursue good and evil at the same time is to divide oneself. The result is hypocrisy and a superficial faith. A person's entire relationship with God is affected, especially in the prayer life.

Double-minded is a word made up of the words "two" and "soul." It refers to a person who is double-minded about something—one whose soul is divided between faith and the world. Such a person "is a walking civil war in which trust and distrust of God wage a continual battle within each other" (William Barclay, *The Letters* of James and Peter [Philadelphia: Westminster, 1976], 46).

Contrast Between Faith and Doubt*

PERSON OF FAITH	PERSON OF DOUBT
Has "faith"	Has "doubt"
Asks for "wisdom"	Does not ask for "wisdom from God" or asks with "doubt"
Receives "wisdom" from God	Receives nothing from God

*Kurt A. Richardson, *James,* The New American Commentary, vol. 36 (Nashville: Broadman & Holman, 1997), 68.

■ *In the midst of trial, the believer must ask for*
■ *an understanding of the purpose behind the*
■ *divine permission of the difficulty. An incen-*
■ *tive to do this is that God will give gener-*
■ *ously to those who ask and will not humiliate*
■ *them for asking. But the believer must not*
■ *ask in doubt, for such an unstable person will*
■ *not receive wisdom from God.*

POVERTY AND WEALTH (1:9–11)

In these three verses James introduced one of the cardinal teachings of the gospel—the theme of reversal.

The Boast of the Poor (v. 9)

Those in the humblest condition should boast in the high position that will be theirs in the future with God. They are to rejoice that God has lifted them up to make His strength perfect in their weakness. The rich, the beautiful, and the strong are to rejoice that God has helped them down from their rickety ladders of self-love. The ground at the foot of the cross is level.

The Reduction of the Rich (vv. 10–11)

The rich are to take pride in their "low position" (v. 10), that is, they should humble themselves now. James was telling the rich that they need to humble themselves against the temptation of trusting in their wealth rather than placing trust in God.

James began to express the full force of his indignation against the injustice perpetrated by the rich against the poor. Again drawing a picture from nature, he said that the rich are like a wild flower, which is an Old Testament image of fragility (Isa. 40:6; Pss. 89:6; 103:15). Under oppressive, scorching heat, its blossom falls, its beauty fades, and the flower withers and dies. Winds coming off the deserts of the south and east were balmy at times, but more often they would sear the land and dry up the vegetation. Like a blast of heat from an oven, this scorching, blistering wind, known as the *Sirocco*, had the power to wither flowers in a matter of minutes. Such is the existence of the rich. "The rich man will fade away even while he goes about his business" (v. 11). He will perish along with all his undertakings. His wealth will prove to be an illusion.

"Many who are first will be last, and many who are last will be first" (Matt. 19:30; cp. Luke 1:46–55).

The church has always been reluctant to hear God's Word about wealth. The words of Jesus on this point are often glossed over. Many people consider James's teaching on the subject offensive. But the context for this hard truth about the wealthy is the instruction James gave to the Christian community. Riches may hold a special status in the world's way of thinking, but in the church, bought by the blood of Jesus Christ, everybody is somebody. Therefore, the wealth and position of the rich are to be carried under an umbrella of humility.

"The wealth of the rich is their fortified wall; they imagine it an unscalable wall" (Prov. 18:11).

Perseveres

This word in Greek is a compound made up of the preposition "under" and the verb "to remain." It means "to remain under" something, and is translated as *endure* or *persevere*. A person who perseveres is one who bears up under something courageously and patiently. It means "to endure, to patiently and triumphantly endure, to show constancy under. It is not the patience which can easily sit down and bow its head and let things descend upon it and passively endure until the storm is passed. It is the spirit which can bear things, not simply with resignation, but with a blazing hope" (Fritz Rienecker, *Linguistic Key to the Greek New Testament* [Grand Rapids: Zondervan, 1980], 723).

■ *Jesus said that "many who are first will be*
■ *last, and many who are last will be first."*
■ *James told his readers that such would be the*
■ *case with the rich. James told the rich that*
■ *they needed to resist the temptation of trust-*
■ *ing in their wealth rather than placing trust*
■ *in God. They were like vulnerable wild flow-*
■ *ers that faded in the scorching heat of the*
■ *desert winds of summer.*

ENDURE TRIALS AND RESIST TEMPTATION (1:12–15)

Trials as Life-Giving (v. 12)

Turning again to the subject of trials, James used the only beatitude of his letter: "Blessed is the man who perseveres under trial, because when he has stood the test, he will receive the crown of life that God has promised to those who love him."

Beatitudes are generally introduced with the term *blessed*. They reflect a person's right relationship to God. We see them in the Old Testament (Deut. 33:29; Pss. 1:1; 2:12; 144:15; Prov. 3:13), and Jesus used them in the Gospel accounts (Matt. 5; 13:16). Because the believer's faithfulness is under trial, James declared such a person "blessed."

For the promised reward, James used the phrase "crown of life." This crown was a head wreath, the victor's prize in the Greek games. It might also be given to the person whom the public wished to honor, and it was worn in religious and secular feasts. The grammar of the text allows for two different renderings of this phrase. It could mean (1) "the crown of life," or

(2) "a living crown," in contrast to a perishable crown. Most translators prefer the former.

Temptations as Life-Taking (vv. 13–15)

Temptations are different from trials. Trials beset us from without. They are an inevitable part of living in a fallen, sin-cursed world. Temptations, however, spring from within when a person is tempted by his or her "own evil desire" (v. 14). James clearly stated that God is not the origin of our temptations. Temptation to sin is the operation of evil forces and the devil.

"Evil desires" are those that originate from within the believer. These may be sexual appetites, the most manipulative, self-gratifying form. Or evil desires may be material goods, money, fame, position, influence, prestige, power, or even comfort. No matter how destructive a sin may be, the believer can find a source of sin outside himself. Our evil desires harbor a reproductive life of their own. Desire conceives an offspring—sin.

The believer must make every effort to resist temptation. For "after desire has conceived, it gives birth to sin; and sin, when it is fully grown, gives birth to death."

Progression of an Uncontrolled Evil Desire

STAGE	
1. Conception	Temptation—the believer is enticed by own evil desires.
2. Birth	Sin—the believer gives way to the evil desire and sin lives in the believer.
3. Maturity	Death—sin become fully grown and eventually slays the host.

■ *James warned believers not to blame God for*
■ *temptation in their lives. God does not dan-*
■ *gle evil before people to entice them to sin. It*
■ *is their own evil desires that lure them to dis-*
■ *obedience. Believers must resist giving in to*
■ *temptation, because it will conceive sin and*
■ *lead to death.*

The Father and the Firstfruits (vv. 16–18)

Because of the complexity of temptation and sin in a believer's life, James was concerned that his readers may have adopted some false ideas about the life of faith. He commanded them, "Don't be deceived, my dear brothers" (v. 16). If they were being deceived, they were to stop. If they had not yet been deceived, they were to beware.

To emphasize that God is not the source of temptation, James proclaimed that God is the source of "every good and perfect gift" (v. 17).

Therefore, the believer is to understand that God is never involved in the evil when we are tempted or enticed by our own desires. Instead, He is the source of good in the believer's life. James described God's gifts as "good and perfect." Such gifts include wisdom (1:5). The Old Testament has much to say about God's good gifts (e.g., Ps. 94:12; Deut. 26:11).

Shadow

"Shadows from the sun shift, but not the One who made the sun!" (J. Ronald Blue from *The Bible Knowledge Commentary* [Victor Books, 822).

James described God as "the Father of the heavenly lights, who does not change like shifting shadows" (v. 17). James was making the point that the Father of lights, who made them all and directs their course, does not change. He is constant, steady, and unchanging. Although the sun, moon, and stars are constantly moving and periodically are concealed, no shadow comes from God.

James concluded this section by contemplating God's "good and perfect" gift of salvation. Certainly, God's supreme good and perfect gift is salvation, the new birth through God's good news in Jesus Christ. James made it clear that believers have faith because God gives them spiritual birth (John 1:13; Phil. 1:29). He clearly contrasted God's action of engendering life with the death that results from allowing sin to conceive in one's life and bring death. This spiritual life is given birth through the "word of truth" that is like a seed that produces a fruit-bearing plant. The word of truth from God, which brought forth the first creation, now brings about the regeneration of human beings.

■ *James taught that God gives only "good and*
■ *perfect" gifts to believers and He will not vary*
■ *from that principle. God's supreme good and*
■ *perfect gift is salvation—the new birth*
■ *through God's good news in Jesus Christ.*

A CORRECT RESPONSE TO GOD'S WORD (1:19–27)

Developing Character (vv. 19–21)

As the life of faith begins with the good gifts of God, so it continues with the development of Christian character. James asked his readers to "take note" of the three exhortations he was about to give them. His first two were references to speech and the tongue.

Be quick to listen. James emphasized listening rather than reacting quickly by speaking.

Wherever wisdom is honored, listening becomes a virtue. Christians are to cultivate the grace of sympathetic listening.

Be slow to speak. In tandem with listening, the believer is to practice the wisdom of careful and deliberate speaking.

Be slow to anger. One's anger may not be completely controllable, but it can be kept in check by avoiding impetuous remarks.

Certainly, believers are not to indulge in temper tantrums. Anger in a believer's life "does not bring about the righteous life that God desires" (v. 20). In other words, God's righteousness cannot be accomplished through human anger.

What [James] means is well illustrated in Jesus' parable of the sower (Mark 4:1–9): the believer has to provide the right climate for the growth of God's word in his life—he has to be fertile "soil." Thus there is need to clear out the weeds of moral filth and evil. James's reference to the word as being planted in us may allude to Jesus' parable, but probably also hints at the fulfillment of Jeremiah's famous prophecy about the new covenant, in which God promised to "put [his] law in their minds and write it on their hearts" (Jer. 31:33) (Douglas Moo in *Evangelical Commentary on the Bible* [Grand Rapids: Baker Book House, 1989, 1,155).

James strongly exhorted his readers to "get rid of all moral filth and . . . evil" (v. 21). All believers need to exercise the spiritual discipline of ferreting out any moral decay in their hearts. Doing so makes room for the "word" that has been implanted in believers. The word James referred to is God's Word that brings salvation in a believer's life. This word continues to grow and mature as believers continue to live committed to the lordship of Jesus. God intends that His children live victorious and abundant lives.

- *Developing character involves the wisdom of*
- *listening and keeping one's anger in check.*
- *The believer is to be rid of all "moral filth*
- *and evil" so he or she can receive the*
- *implanted word and allow it to take root.*

Putting Faith to Work (vv. 22–27)

Do the word. Because the implanted word is dynamic, working salvation in the believers' lives, it is imperative that they "do what it says" (v. 22). Those who only hear the word but do not do it are deceiving themselves, James declared.

James went on to use figures of speech to describe the function of the word in the believer's life.

The Word Is a Mirror (vv. 23–24). James used the illustration of a person looking intently into the mirror. This "mirror" concept is the reader's key for understanding this section of James's letter.

James implied two mistakes that occur when the believer fails to act upon the word: (1) the believer doesn't treat the truth of the word as reality; and (2) the believer ignores the message of the word.

The Word Is the Perfect Law (v. 25). The law is "perfect" in the sense that it participates in God's goodness and is essential to His gifts bestowed in wisdom upon believers. James told his readers that it is "the law that gives freedom." This combination of law and freedom brings to mind the apostle Paul's theology of the believer's freedom in Christ (see Rom. 6:18–22; 2 Cor. 3:17; Gal. 2:4; 5:1, 13–14; 6:2).

Mirrors in Ancient Literature

In the ancient world, the *mirror*, a specially shaped piece of polished metal, was used to inspect or decorate a person's body. The ancient literature is replete with references to the mirror and its use as a metaphor for moral development (Kurt A. Richardson, *James,* The New American Commentary, vol. 36 [Nashville: Broadman & Holman, 1997], 95–96).

How God's Word Helps Believers

FIGURE OF SPEECH	PASSAGE	LESSON
Seed	v. 21	The implanted word works out salvation in the believer.
Mirror	vv. 23–24	The word reflects the believer's spiritual condition.
Law	v. 25	The perfect law of God sets the believer free.

James closed this section of his letter by writing that those who do the will of God according to His word will be blessed.

■ *It is imperative that believers not only hear the*
■ *word implanted in them, but that they do what*
■ *it says. James presented three figures of speech*
■ *that explain how God's Word helps the*
■ *believer: (1) a seed that could be planted with a*
■ *Christian to grow into salvation; (2) a mirror*
■ *that clearly reflects the condition of the one*
■ *looking into it; and (3) a law that provides free-*
■ *dom.*

WORTHLESS RELIGION AND GENUINE RELIGION (1:26–27)

Worthless Religion (v. 26)

A person who imagines himself to be religious while avoiding discipline that is required to "keep a tight rein on his tongue" has fallen prey to self-deception. One characteristic of self-deception in the believer's life is an empty show of religious devotion. James taught that such religion is "worthless."

Genuine Religion (v. 27)

Genuine religion is "pure and faultless," thrusting the believer into the real world of struggles, tears, broken relationships, and raging animosities. This kind of religion involves itself in practical care for "orphans and widows in their distress."

The Christian must always be cautious to avoid compromise with the world. James used the graphic term *polluted* to make this point. This word refers to the ongoing practice of staying free of contamination from the ungodly attitudes and actions of the world.

- *James contrasted what is worthless religion*
- *with what is genuine. Those who practice*
- *worthless religion have fallen prey to*
- *self-deception. Those who practice genuine*
- *religion are careful to avoid being polluted*
- *by the world.*

A true response to God's Word is both outward activity and inward control. Ministry to orphans and widows is the outward activity. Separation from the world is evidence of inner control.

QUESTIONS TO GUIDE YOUR STUDY

1. According to James, what is the purpose of trials in the life of the believer?
2. James exhorted his readers to ask God for wisdom. How were they to go about doing so? What does it mean to be "double-minded?"
3. What were James's commands to the poor? To the rich? How were they to respond to his teaching?
4. James said much about temptation in the life of the believer. What is the source of temptation? What happens when a believer gives in to temptation?

James opens this chapter with a warning. It serves as an intentional break and signals the beginning of four exhortations on authentic faith.

In this chapter James shows how believers should live out their faith in relation to others within the body of believers. For James, faith and works are inseparable. He sets forth three arguments in support of his position.

James's Three Arguments in Chapter 2

PASSAGE	ARGUMENT
2:1–7	Authentic faith does not play favorites.
2:8–13	The "royal law" is "love your neighbor as yourself."
2:14–25	Faith must have deeds.

DO NOT SHOW FAVORITISM (2:1–7)

The Glorious Christ (v. 1)
People play favorites, but God doesn't. In the opening verse of chapter 2, James told his readers, "Don't show favoritism." Playing favorites or showing partiality is incompatible with the ways of Christ.

The word translated "favoritism" is a compound word and is a distinctive Christian word. It is made up of the words *face* or *person* and *to lay hold of*. Having its roots in the Old Testament, it is a Hebrew idiom meaning "to lift up the face on a person," or "to be favorable and so partial."

Favoritism becomes a fault when a person responsible to give judgment gives respect to a person's position, popularity, or circumstances instead of that person's intrinsic conditions. In the Old Testament, evil judges often showed favoritism toward rich and powerful people at the expense of those who were not (see Ps. 82:2; Prov. 18:5; Mal. 2:9). This behavior or attitude is *not* characteristic of God. See this word used in this sense of partiality (respect of persons) in Rom. 2:11; Col. 3:25; and Eph. 6:9 (taken from A. T. Robertson, *Word Pictures in the New Testament*, vol. 6, "General Epistles and Revelation of John," 27, and *Vine's Complete Expository Dictionary of Old and New Testament Words* [Nashville: Thomas Nelson, 1996], 469).

There is a strong affinity between what James wrote in this passage and Lev. 19:15: "You shall do no injustice in judgment; you shall not be partial to the poor nor defer to the great, but you are to judge your neighbor fairly" (NASB).

When a Christian shows favoritism, he is being double-minded. A Christian has identified with Jesus and His interests and concerns. Jesus, God's unique Son, chose to identify with the poor and helpless during His ministry on earth. His attitude is the model for every believer. So when a Christian plays favorites, he's at odds with his Lord.

An Illustration of Favoritism (vv. 2–4)

To drive home his point, James gave a case study of favoritism (v. 1). It may well be not just a hypothetical case but something he actually observed in the churches.

Taking this parable to heart is painful for many believers and congregations. Although the gospel requires a change in social relations within the church, in contemporary Western middle-class churches, the poor rarely would visit. The church needs to refrain from favoritism based on economic, educational, and social status and practice the redemptive role given God's people by Christ. Moving from favoritism to fairness will please Christ and will raise the credibility of the church in the community in which it is planted.

The illustration presents two church visitors and an usher. The usher favors the high-class visitor and provides him with a "good seat" but relegates the low-class visitor to a position of inferiority and humiliation: "Sit on the floor by my feet." For the members of this congregation, the visit of the rich man became a test of their Christian faith. Sadly, they didn't pass this test.

The church of Jesus
Christ must live by the
principles of Christ
rather than those of
the world.

Contrasts Between the Rich Man and Poor Man

RICH MAN	POINT OF CONTRAST	POOR MAN
Well-dressed ("fine clothes")	Attire	Unsightly ("shabby clothes")
Required preferential treatment	Attitude	Expected fair treatment
Favored	Treatment	Discriminated against

GOD'S DISCRIMINATION (2:5–7)

James followed his illustration with the emphatic words, "Listen, my dear brothers." He wanted his readers' attention, for he was ready to give them a statement of truth about God's discrimination. He framed this section with a series of rhetorical questions:

Rhetorical Question

A question asked primarily for effect and not expecting an answer.

- "Has not God chosen those who are poor in the eyes of the world to be rich in faith and to inherit the kingdom he promised those who love him?" (v. 5).

- "Is it not the rich who are exploiting you? Are they not the ones who are dragging you into court?" (v. 6).

- "Are they not the ones who are slandering the noble name of him to whom you belong?" (v. 7).

The expected though unexpressed answer to these questions is *yes.* James told his readers that they had insulted the poor and honored the rich. They had disregarded the honor that God bestows upon the poor. In addition, they had failed to confront the rich for depriving others of what was due them.

James made two important statements about the poor:

1. *The poor believers are made wealthy in faith.* God chooses to make the poor heirs of the treasures of the kingdom that cannot perish. Bestowing these eternal treasures is beyond human ability. Only God can do this.

We are reminded of the words of our Lord in Luke 6:20: "Blessed are you who are poor, for yours is the kingdom of God."

2. *The poor are heirs of the kingdom of God.* God especially delights in raising the poor from where they are to be His sons and daughters.

To be heirs of God's kingdom is to become His children and to share in His nature through resurrection. Jesus is saying that the poor are God's prime subjects of this inheritance in Christ. The church of Christ is to make every effort to ennoble the poor and to rejoice in salvation together with them.

Most of us know how it feels to be on the wrong end of favoritism. It doesn't feel good. Remembering how it feels, and practicing the Royal Law, we will avoid showing partiality when dealing with others—regardless of their station in life.

■ *Favoritism is a complex sin—an evil—that*
■ *leads to division within the fellowship of*
■ *believers. James commanded his readers to*
■ *refrain from demonstrating favoritism to the*
■ *rich who attended their services while ignor-*
■ *ing the poor, for God has chosen the poor to*
■ *be wealthy in faith and heirs of His kingdom.*
■ *The church of Jesus Christ must unite around*
■ *the principles of Christ rather than follow*
■ *the practices of the world.*

THE ROYAL LAW (2:8–13)

The Excellent Deed (v. 8)
James argued that rather than showing favoritism, Christians are to follow the Royal Law. Echoing the words of Jesus, James defined this law as "Love your neighbor as yourself" (v. 8).

Teachings on The Royal Law

JESUS	JAMES	PAUL
"Love your neighbor as yourself" (Matt. 22:39).	"Love your neighbor as yourself" (James 2:8).	"The only thing that counts is faith expressing itself through love" (Gal. 5:6).

Offensive at Every Point (vv. 9–11)
At this point, James forestalled our responding to him by saying something like, "Favoritism isn't all that bad. It's so common, it couldn't be too bad."

James then made a strong claim. If a person fails to keep even the small points of the law, they break God's entire law.

He illustrated this claim with an example. If a person doesn't commit adultery but murders someone, he breaks the entire law.

A key point to gain from this section is that God's law exposes sin and its true nature. Sin in a person's life is never a question of breaking a single command, but rather of violating the integrity of the whole law.

The Freedom-Giving Law (vv. 12–13)

James stirred his readers into action by commanding them to "speak and act" (v. 12) as those who are going to be judged by the law. Both of those words speak of ongoing actions or habits (see A. T. Robertson, *Word Pictures in the New Testament*, vol. 6, "General Epistles and Revelation of John," 33). James closed this section on the Royal Law with two main points.

The Christian lives under the law of liberty. What does it mean to live under the law of liberty? This is the second time (1:25) this phrase, "the law that gives freedom," occurs in James. From the perspective of sinful human beings, any kind of law seems like a burden—especially at those points where the law opposes what we want to do at the moment.

From the Christian's point of view, the law looks different. We now see that living our life in harmony with God's law is the way of joy and fulfillment. It's like a train running on the tracks for which it was designed rather than running off in fields and forests. Conversion gives us the power and the desire to live as God made us. This is the law of liberty.

Coming back to the problem of favoritism, we might say that it's in our interest not to hurt other people by showing favoritism. We're following the law of liberty when we treat others as we want to be treated.

He who shows mercy will find mercy. James's statement about impending judgment is harsh: "Judgment without mercy will be shown to anyone who has not been merciful" (v. 13).

Jesus was clear in His teaching on this truth:

Matthew 6:14–15: "For if you forgive men when they sin against you, your heavenly Father will also forgive you. But if you do not forgive men their sins, your Father will not forgive your sins."

Matthew 7:1–2: "Do not judge, or you too will be judged. For in the same way you judge others, you will be judged, and with the measure you use, it will be measured to you."

Mercy is a very important ingredient in human relationships because it is a direct indicator of how much we're aware of God's forgiveness of us.

In verse 13 James offered one of the highest principles in all of Scripture: "Mercy triumphs over judgment." On judgment day, God will reserve His judgment where merciful faith is evident. His will to condemn will be emptied by His will to show mercy, and judgment will be swallowed up in mercy.

"... mercy should be the mark of a regenerated person. If it is present in a believer's life, he will have nothing to fear at the judgment" (*Expositor's Bible Commentary*, vol. 12 [The Zondervan corporation, 1981], 180).

■ *James supplied the antidote to wrong think-*
■ *ing and false judgments of the rich: "Love*
■ *your neighbor as yourself." To play favorites*
■ *is to commit sin, and breaking the law on this*
■ *point is very serious business. Instead,*
■ *believers are to "speak" and "act" as those*
■ *who will be judged by the law. Those who*
■ *show no mercy will be judged harshly. James*
■ *assured the Christian that in the grace of*
■ *God "mercy triumphs over judgment."*

FAITH MUST HAVE DEEDS (2:14–26)

This passage is the third argument of this chapter, delivering the true content of faith according to James. Demonstrating the authenticity of faith is its primary focus.

The relationship between faith and works has been the cause of debate and division among Christians since the first century. Verses 14–26 have been a battlefield for this controversy. The great reformer Martin Luther found this portion of James's letter especially objectionable to his understanding of salvation and faith.

Although James's and Paul's teachings seem to be in conflict at this point, it can be shown that they are consistent with each other.

James and Paul approached faith and works from different points of view. James had a viewpoint that was essentially pastoral. Paul's viewpoint was essentially missionary. James saw faith and works in light of what God requires of those who have already become Christians, while Paul saw faith and works in the light of what God requires for a person to become a Christian.

This portion of God's truth (2:14–26) can deliver Christians from the false dichotomy that mistakenly assumes a conflict between faith and works in the lives of God's people.

USAGE OF THE TERMS *FAITH*, *WORKS*, AND *JUSTIFICATION* BY JAMES AND PAUL

TERM	JAMES	PAUL
Faith	The giving of intellectual assent to the facts of Christianity, an assent that was barren of good works, inactive, and therefore, useless.	Saving faith in Jesus Christ, which faith issues normally and naturally in works of righteousness.
Works	Acts of ministry, mercy, love, and justice done in obedience to the demands of God's indwelling Spirit.	Acts performed legalistically in obedience to the letter of the law in order to earn salvation.
Justification	The believer's final acceptance by God at the last judgment.	God's immediate acceptance of any sinner who repented and believed in obedience to the call of the gospel.

An Open Question (v. 14)

James presented an example and then asked a rhetorical question. Let's suppose a person says that he has faith but has no works. James asked, "Can such faith save him?"

The answer he expected is *no*.

Need Without Deed (vv. 15–16)

This illustration from James is like a Christian meeting a needy person in his or her fellowship, but responding with a "have a nice day!" or "good luck!" and moving on. Such "faith" lacks Christian action. We see a similar issue in 1 John 3:17–18: "If anyone has material possessions and sees a brother in need but has no pity on him, how can the love of God be in him? Dear children, let us not love with words or tongue but with actions and in truth."

At this point, James brought a strong illustration to bear. Suppose a brother or sister in Christ lacks food or clothing. Suppose further that a person thought to be a Christian tells this needy person, "God bless you. Go in peace. Be clothed and fed," without raising a finger to help the person find warmth and food.

A Pronouncement of Faith's Death (v. 17)

James concluded that this is dead faith. It's dead because it shows no signs of life. The kind of faith that James is criticizing is mere words. Apparently, this was a problem in James's day. Some people were equating faith with the simple verbal claim that they had faith. These claims apart from works were not the real thing.

A Question of Proof (vv. 18–19)

Perhaps Christians had come to see some believers in the church as having faith and others as people of works. James didn't allow this as a valid dichotomy. For James, faith is shown in and by works.

Let's suppose a person believes that God exists, James declared. This belief isn't faith. After all, the demons not only believe but they know that God exists and they shudder at the thought of God. But they don't have faith. They are against God. Authentic faith is something more than belief. What could it be?

Faith and Deeds (v. 20)

James began this section of his argument by saying once again to his imagined opponent, "Do you want evidence that faith without deeds is useless?"

He then proceeded to deliver the answer. In these next few verses James provided two examples of a faith evidenced by works. He used two Old Testament characters: Abraham and Rahab.

The Example of Abraham (vv. 20–24)

God commanded Abraham (Genesis 22) to take his only son Isaac to the land of Moriah. On one of the mountains there, he was to offer his son as a burnt offering. Abraham proceeded to act according to God's command. James saw Abraham's belief in God and his action as working together. Abraham's action made his faith in God complete.

James asked rhetorically, "Was not our ancestor Abraham considered righteous for what he did?" He assumed we will answer *yes*.

What's the relationship of this claim with Paul's teaching that we are justified by faith alone apart from the deeds of the law (Rom. 3:27–28)? Both James and Paul used the same Greek word for *justify*. Both James and Paul appealed to Abraham's action to support their very different claims.

The supposed conflict between James and Paul involves the use of some of the same key words: *justify*, *faith*, and *works*. Let's look more closely.

James (2:23) quotes Genesis 15:6: "Abraham believed God, and it was credited to him as righteousness." James then declared (v. 24), "You see that a person is justified by what he does and not by faith alone."

Brought to completion (NRSV)

This is one word in the Greek text, and it means "to bring to completion, to bring to maturity, to perfect, to consummate." "As the tree is perfected by its fruits, so faith by its works. Works do not animate faith; but faith produces works, and works perfect faith. Faith itself 'is perfected,' that is, shown to be true, by works" (Fritz Rienecker, *Linguistic Key to the Greek New Testament* [Grand Rapids: Zondervan, 1980], 731).

Compare what Paul said: "For we maintain that a man is justified by faith apart from observing the law" (Rom. 3:28).

Paul and James were dealing with two different situations. Apparently, the kind of faith James had encountered was *belief that* rather than *belief in*. There's a vast difference between the two. The demons *believe that* God exists, but they don't *believe in* or trust in God.

For Paul, faith included *belief that* but he added to it *belief in* to the point of obedience. Paul saw faith resulting in good works. It's likely Paul would agree with James that good works give evidence of faith. But Paul maintained that works of the law—merely human effort—do not make a person right before God. God justifies. Humans receive what God has done by faith. Good deeds follow from saving faith.

The Example of Rahab (v. 25)

James turned to the example of "Rahab the prostitute." In James's day, prostitutes were ranked with tax collectors among the lowest class of people. James used such a person to underscore his emphasis on vital, useful faith. We find Rahab's story in Josh. 2:1–21. She mercifully hid the Israelite spies from her own countrymen and cared for their needs before the destruction of Jericho. She exemplified faith in that she recognized the truth of God in His works of delivering Israel, and she demonstrated that faith. It is for her faith that she is remembered (see Heb. 11:31).

There Is No Faith Without Deeds (v. 26)

James closed this chapter by reemphasizing verse 17, which is the beginning of the current portion of his letter begun at verse 17, stating that "as the body without the spirit is dead, so

All believers need to nurture a living faith that issues in works of righteousness to the glory of God and the advancement of Christ's kingdom. This means that believers demonstrate their faith by doing what God requires.

faith without deeds is dead." He used the image
of a corpse to emphasize a lifeless faith.

■ *Demonstrating the authenticity of faith was*
■ *James's focus in this section. For him, a liv-*
■ *ing faith cannot be disjoined from deeds that*
■ *are evidence of that faith. James used the*
■ *illustration of Abraham, whose faith was*
■ *made complete by his obedient actions.*
■ *Because of his faith, God "credited" it to him*
■ *as righteousness. Justification from God*
■ *comes to those who put faith to work and*
■ *who perceive that faith and works are the*
■ *two sides of the coin of God's saving grace.*

QUESTIONS TO GUIDE YOUR STUDY

1. Why is it sin to show favoritism?
2. James wrote about the Royal Law. What is it? What is its application to modern-day believers?
3. What is the nature of the faith which James described? What is the relationship between faith and works?
4. What was the main point of James's illustrations of Abraham and Rahab?

We all know what damage can be done by false-hoods, gossip, and degrading, abusive language. James insisted that Christians obey God by controlling their tongues and all of their desires. The tongue has power for both good and evil. Characteristics of the tongue include stubbornness and inconsistency. In this chapter James urged his readers to demonstrate heavenly wisdom rather than earthly folly.

THE RESPONSIBILITY OF TEACHERS (3:1)

In the early church, teachers were important people. Wherever genuine teachers are mentioned, it is with honor. Teachers who failed in their responsibilities were considered false teachers (Acts 15:24; Rom. 2:17–29).

Teachers in the New Testament

Instruction, or the gift of teaching, is one of the abilities God gives certain Christians to equip them to serve in the Christian community. Teachers were those who provided instruction and exhortation on aspects of Christian life and thought, and directed to persons who had already made a faith commitment. Instruction is frequently distinguished from evangelistic preaching.

A teacher was one who held something of an office within the church (Acts 13:1; 1 Cor. 12:28; Eph. 4:11; 2 Tim. 1:11). He was a person who had mastered the Scriptures and how they were to be applied to faith and life. The teacher's primary tool was speech, and its instrument was the tongue.

The church's teaching ministry has several dimensions.

The church teaches about Jesus. The church presents the basic details of Jesus' life and ministry: His death, burial, and resurrection. It helps members understand the meaning of these events for all time.

The church teaches spirituality. New Christians are not to remain "babes in Christ," but to increase in "grace, and in knowledge" of the Lord Jesus Christ (2 Pet. 3:18). Christian spirituality is the process of growing in faith. In its teaching ministry, the church guides Christians in the life of faith through prayer, Bible study, and spiritual reflection.

The church teaches Christian ethics. Those who follow Christ must be conformed to His image. The church instructs its members in faithfulness, morality, honesty, and integrity. Ethical instruction is not focused on legalism but on a way of life according to Christ's new commandment to love one another (John 13:34–35). Jesus is the ultimate moral teacher and example for the people of God.

The church instructs in Christian doctrine. The church teaches the basic truths of the Christian faith. It guides Christians in understanding significant beliefs. It opens the Scriptures to determine those doctrinal ideals upon which the church is founded.

As the church teaches, it also evangelizes. The teaching ministry of the church is another way in which the people of God declare their faith in order that others may know Christ and grow up in Him. It is no wonder that James warned teachers to control the primary instrument of their vocation—the tongue.

James was not trying to recruit as many teachers as possible. He said plainly that not many people should become teachers because teachers are judged more strictly than others.

Teaching has great potential to build up individual believers and the church. At the same time, wrongful teaching can be destructive.

We want workers who build airplanes to be well taught. We want physicians to be taught by those who know what they're talking about. How much more should we expect competency from those who teach concerning issues with eternal consequences?

$\sf S_N$

- *In New Testament times, a teacher was a*
- *person who had mastered the Scriptures and*
- *how they were to be applied to faith and life.*
- *The teacher's primary tool was speech, and*
- *its instrument was the tongue. James warned*
- *teachers to control the tongue, for they would*
- *be judged more strictly for its use.*

THE UNCONTROLLABLE TONGUE (3:2–12)

The tongue receives major attention in the Bible. The tongue was thought of as expressing a person's true nature since speech was viewed as more than just a verbal phenomenon (Pss. 64:2–3; 45:1; Prov. 10:20; 17:20). The wisdom writings of the Old Testament emphasized the practical results of the use of the tongue (Prov. 12:18; 18:21; 21:6; 21:23; 25:23; 26:28). Like a bit in a horse's mouth or the rudder of a ship, the tongue could control the direction of a person's life (James 3:3–8). Since the tongue reveals what is in a person's heart, its use has ethical consequences, whether good or bad (Pss. 34:13; 37:30; 109:2; 120:2; 140:2–3; Isa. 59:3).

The tongue was considered an organ of the body which played a central role in the expression of a person's religious commitment. The tongue could be used to praise God (Pss. 35:28; 51:14; 71:24; Rom. 14:11; Phil. 2:11). On the other hand, the tongue could cause separation from God (Job 15:4–5; Pss. 39:1; 78:35–37). The potential for good or bad, which is a part of human nature, is actualized through the tongue (James 3:9–10).

The tongue is influential in all human relationships. Its strength is out of proportion to its size, and it has an almost limitless potential for good or bad. In verses 2–12 James presented several analogies regarding the tongue to describe its nature and potential.

Analogies of Size (vv. 2–5)

James commented that "the tongue is a small part of the body, but it makes great boasts" (v. 5). Here he delivered for his readers three analogies that illustrate how small things can have control over large things, relating those to the nature of the tongue.

A Horse's Bit (v. 3). Bits are placed in the mouths of big horses to direct them. With this small bit, the rider controls the entire horse. James's analogy provides a clear connection between the turning, or controlling, of the "whole animal" with a bit, and the controlling of the "whole body" with the tongue (v. 2).

Just as a rider can control a horse, so a person can control his or her willfulness and appetites.

A Ship's Rudder (v. 4). Small rudders are used by pilots to guide large ships. A ship is an excellent illustration of bringing under control a very large object with a small but effective instrument. The analogy is heightened by the fact that on the open sea, and against the wind, a vessel without a rudder is uncontrollable. Such a ship is driven and tossed about by the waves that move it along (James 1:6).

Just as a rudder in the hands of the trained pilot can steer a vessel through the harshest of winds, the Christian who wisely controls the tongue can direct the potential and impact of his or her speech.

A Spark in the Forest (v. 5). Although deceptively small and seemingly insignificant, a small spark has potential for massive destruction. One small, unattended spark in the forest can kindle a fire of great force. Many forest fires have been caused by careless campers who failed to douse that last single spark, which then grew into an uncontrollable inferno after being fanned by the wind.

Just as a small spark can lead to a great fire of destruction, a word or words of boasting from the tongue can reap much destruction.

- *James wrote that "the tongue is a small part*
- *of the body, but it makes great boasts" (v. 5).*
- *In this section he delivered three analogies*
- *that illustrate how small things can have*
- *control over large things, and he related*
- *those to the nature of the tongue.*

Analogies of Force (vv. 6–8)

James turned next to two analogies of force regarding the tongue: It is a fire and an uncontrollable animal. These become forces of corruption and destruction. James was clear that the tongue cannot be tamed; it must be kept in check.

The tongue is a fire, "a world of evil," with far-reaching consequences. The person who fails in the area of speech certainly will fail in actions.

Fire (v. 6). James wrote that the tongue is a "fire" that corrupts the whole person. The tongue is set on fire by hell itself. "In a most powerful image, the fire that is the little tongue, a little spark causing great fires, has another fire that causes it. Hell has outcroppings in the world, and one of them is evil speaking" (Kurt A. Richardson, *James*, The New American Commentary, vol. 36 [Nashville: Broadman & Holman, 1997], 154).

To show the extent of its potential, James set forth three cause-and-effect relationships of the tongue as a fire:

In contrast to man's ability to control and tame animals, he has failed to tame the tongue. As a result, the tongue constantly must be kept under the lordship of Jesus Christ.

1. Corrupt speech corrupts the whole body.
2. The corrupted body sets in motion the evil course of an entire life.
3. The destructiveness of evil speech is derived from the destructiveness of hell.

An Uncontrollable Animal (vv. 7–8). We have tamed all kinds of creatures from the animal world, but humans generally fail to tame the tongue. "It is a restless evil, full of deadly poison," James declared. "This does not mean that for Christians our talk is uncontrollable. It means that the tongue needs everlasting supervision, that it can never be trusted completely, that it can never be left alone without careful direction from the morally responsible and socially sensitive people of God" (Foy Valentine, *Hebrews, James, 1 & 2 Peter,* Layman's Bible Book Commentary, vol. 23 [Nashville: Broadman & Holman Publishers, 1981], 83).

■ *James offered two analogies of force regard-*
■ *ing the tongue: It is a fire and an uncontrol-*
■ *lable animal. These become forces of*
■ *corruption and destruction. James was clear*
■ *that the tongue cannot be tamed; it must be*
■ *kept in check.*

Analogies of Incompatibility (vv. 9–12)

At the outset of these verses, James referred to the fact that men and women have been made in the image of God, "God's likeness" (v. 9). Every human has the stamp of God's likeness. James's point here was that God's image in others is to be respected and not made the object of malediction. To dishonor others is to dishonor God.

James continued his pattern of analogies with three analogies of incompatibility.

*Praise and Cursing (v. 10).*The tongue has the capacity both to give praise and to curse. The obvious question that arises is, How can speech that builds up and speech that tears down come from the same mouth?

Full of deadly poison

The word *deadly* is a compound term made up of two words: the noun "death" and the verb "to bring." The word describes something that *is death-bringing.* In this case, the death-bringing agent is poison. It is used only here in the New Testament. "Like the restless death-bringing tongue of the asp before it strikes" (A. T. Robertson, *Word Pictures in the New Testament,* vol. 6, "General Epistles and Revelation of John," 44).

Just as a spring that produces fresh water will not produce salty water, the source of the believer's speech should produce "fresh" or wholesome speech.

Fresh Water and Salt Water (v. 11). Fresh water corresponds to water that is good or desirable, such as for bathing, drinking, or irrigating crops. Salt water corresponds to water that is bad or undesirable. Salt water is unfit for drinking, irrigating, or bathing.

Fruit Trees and Their Fruit (v. 12). James closed his series of analogies with two illustrations about the fig tree and the grapevine. Rather than presenting a contrast here, he focused on the natural order of living things: Fig trees produce figs, not olives, and grapevines produce grapes, not figs. The believer's speech is a revelation of his or her character. A person's speech comes from the heart.

More friendships are broken, more families are divided, and more churches are split by what is said than by what is done. Foy Valentine observed, "A fist can only reach three feet, but the tongue is an intercontinental ballistic missile" (Foy Valentine, *Hebrews, James, 1 & 2 Peter*, Layman's Bible Book Commentary, vol. 23 [Nashville: Broadman & Holman Publishers, 1981], 83).

Believers are to avoid the temptation to speak evil against others.

■ *James provided two more analogies that*
■ *were based on incompatibilities. The lessons*
■ *for his readers were that believers are to be*
■ *careful in their speech in order to avoid*
■ *evil-speaking. Speech should be wholesome*
■ *and from the heart.*

THE TWO "WISDOMS" (3:13–15)

The Nature of Heavenly Wisdom (v. 13)

In the passage that covers 3:13–4:10, James focused on two main ideas: those who are friends of *God* and those who are friends of the *world*. Those who are friends of God embrace heavenly wisdom; those who are friends of the world embrace "earthly, unspiritual" wisdom. His opening rhetorical question asked his readers to take inventory of themselves and determine which wisdom was guiding them.

James coupled the terms *wise* and *understanding* to describe people who embrace heavenly wisdom. Such people measure up to God's standards with both attitudes and proper behavior. In addition, the coupling of these two words views not only the objective truth, but also the application of the truth.

THE COOPERATION OF WISDOM AND
UNDERSTANDING

Wisdom	Understanding
Knows how to do good	Knows why wisdom is good
Concerned with the conduct of one's life	Involves the demonstration of a good life

Wisdom that comes from God leads a person in a life that grows in understanding. The "word of truth" (James 1:18), which is implanted in the believer's heart, becomes a primary source of God's wisdom. Kurt Richardson explains the process:

"Wisdom in the life of the believer advances in cycles. Wisdom entails understanding, which entails the demonstration of a good life, which entails humble deeds, which entail wisdom. True wisdom constantly engenders a cycle of increasing virtue that continues throughout a lifetime. The seed of the Word of God grows within and grows up in a believer according to the standard of well-being and well-doing established for us by God" (*James,* The New American Commentary, vol. 36 [Nashville: Broadman & Holman, 1997], 163).

The word *wise* comes from the term that describes "the wisdom of ultimate things" and "knowledge of the most exalted subjects." It speaks of wisdom that is divine in nature and origin. In Matt. 23:34, we see Jesus sending out "wise men" who were experienced and knowledgeable in the things of God. This word *wise* is the technical term for "teacher." The Jewish use of this word spoke of a person who has a knowledge of practical, moral wisdom, resting on the knowledge of God. It is in contrast to the Greek philosophical term that meant "theoretical wisdom" (taken from Fritz Rienecker, *Linguistic Key to the Greek New Testament* [Grand Rapids: Zondervan, 1980], 734; and William Barclay, *New Testament Words* [Philadelphia: Westminster, 1974], 258–59).

"Wisdom does not show itself so much in precept as in life."
Senca

■ *Heavenly wisdom involves both wisdom and*
■ *understanding—knowing the truth and act-*
■ *ing on it. Those who embrace heavenly wis-*
■ *dom measure up to God's standards with*
■ *both their attitudes and their conduct.*

The Nature of Earthly Wisdom (vv. 14–15)

James sharply contrasted heavenly wisdom with earthly wisdom. The word *but* indicates a contrast of values and definition with heavenly wisdom. He describes earthly wisdom as "of the devil." Signs of this wisdom in the life of a person are "bitter envy" and "selfish ambition." James made a contrast between the Word of God growing in the heart of the believer who embraces heavenly wisdom and the envy and selfish ambition that grows within the person who embraces earthly wisdom.

James provided his readers with more information about this earthy wisdom.

It is unspiritual. Rather than taking hold of the gifts of God and anticipating the joy that is to come, this wisdom is very self-centered and oriented to personal gain. It is concerned only with physical needs and urges and is driven by the dictates of the selfish mind and heart.

It is demonic. The phrase "of the devil" is the Greek word for "demonic." "The demonic is an umbrella description for both the directly satanic and all human opposition to God and his Spirit. Thus, the faith that merely assents to gospel truths is on par with demonic faith (2:19b). As soon as believers act out of wrath, they are no longer serving God and so are opposed to God (1:20)" (Kurt A. Richardson, *James,* The New American Commentary, vol. 36 [Nashville: Broadman & Holman, 1997], 167).

The believer needs to be alert and careful not to allow a foothold for earthly wisdom. The tongue is influenced strongly by such unspiritual and demonic wisdom.

Bitter envy

The phrase "bitter envy" translates one Greek word that is sometimes rendered "zeal" or "bitter jealousy." The idea here is of a fierce desire to promote one's own opinion to the exclusion of others.

"There is a way that seems right to a man, but in the end it leads to death." (Prov. 14:12).

■ *James sharply contrasted heavenly wisdom*
■ *with earthly wisdom. The signs of earthly wis-*
■ *dom in the life of a person are bitter envy and*
■ *selfish ambition. The believer is not to allow a*
■ *place for such wisdom in his or her life.*

THE TWO WISDOMS AND THEIR HARVESTS (3:16–18)

In the last three verses of this chapter, James categorized the characteristics of the two wisdoms, focusing primarily on the virtues of true, heavenly wisdom.

The Harvest of Earthly Wisdom (v. 16)

Disorder. This word is also translated "confusion." It carries with it the ideas of trouble, disturbance, and instability. In political contexts it means "anarchy."

Every Evil Practice. The NRSV translates this phrase as "wickedness of every kind." James did not teach that believers who return to earthly wisdom become experts in all kinds of evil. What was likely in his mind here is that when believers return to earthly wisdom, which is demonic and unspiritual, anything can happen. People fueled by ambition and this kind of wisdom will do whatever it takes.

The Harvest of Heavenly Wisdom (vv. 17–18)

Pure. This term speaks of sincere, moral, and spiritual integrity.

Peace-Loving. A person governed by true wisdom is one who promotes peace.

Considerate of Others. The believer's example is the gentleness exhibited by the Lord Jesus

Christ. The process of spreading the good news is not to be mixed with harshness or anger.

Submissive. This kind of person is compliant, approachable, and willing to yield—one who willingly receives instruction about the truth.

Merciful. This can involve forgiving others or acting generously toward others in need.

Bears Good Fruit. To James, being merciful and bearing good fruit were nearly synonymous. Good deeds are the fruit of righteousness.

Impartial. An impartial person is one who does not waiver in the way he or she relates to others. For James, this word was the opposite of double-mindedness, a condition he wrote about frequently.

Sincere. This refers to a person of integrity who exhibits a singleness of heart. His speech and actions are consistent, and they do not betray each other. This kind of person is without hypocrisy and pretense.

Selfish ambition

This phrase is one word in the Greek text, meaning the vice of a leader of a party created for his own pride. It is "pushing forward for one's personal ends, partisanship" (A. T. Robertson, *Word Pictures in the New Testament,* vol. 6, "General Epistles and Revelation of John," 46). It is partly ambition; partly rivalry. (Fritz Rienecker, *Linguistic Key to the Greek New Testament* [Grand Rapids: Zondervan, 1980], 734–35).

James's Contrast Between Earthly Wisdom and Heavenly Wisdom

	ELEMENTS	RESULT
EARTHLY WISDOM:	Envious Selfish ambition	Disorder and every evil practice
HEAVENLY WISDOM	Purity Peacemaking Consideration of others Merciful Good fruit Impartial Sincere	A harvest of righteousness

"A church that is rich in reconciling activities, that is, evangelism, the defense of the poor, counseling the troubled, offering hospitality to the stranger, providing shelter for the battered, sending gospel missionaries throughout the world, and many more, certainly reaps a rich harvest of righteousness. Whenever the church of Christ is doing these things, the kingdom of God is evidence. This harvest precisely is what Jesus meant by the admonition to 'seek first the kingdom of God and its righteousness' (Matt. 6:33)" (Kurt A. Richardson, *James*, The New American Commentary, vol. 36 [Nashville: Broadman & Holman, 1997], 172).

■ *James focused on the differing harvests of the*
■ *two wisdoms. Earthly wisdom yields disor-*
■ *der and all kind of evil, whereas heavenly*
■ *wisdom produces a harvest of righteousness.*

QUESTIONS TO GUIDE YOUR STUDY

1. What responsibility did James assign to teachers of God's Word? Describe the church's ministry of teaching.
2. Why did James place such an emphasis on the use of the tongue?
3. What do James's analogies about the tongue and speech teach us? What truths especially stand out for you?
4. Contrast the two wisdoms. What is the product of each?

- - - - - - -

The break between chapters 3 and 4 falls in the midst of the first part of James's letter (3:13–4:10). The first part of this chapter (vv. 1–10), therefore, is a continuation of his theme about the two kinds of wisdom and how they play out in a person's life.

In this chapter James depicted the issues of right and wrong in a context outside the church. In addition to urging ethical action, James warned about conflicts that result in quarrels and fights. His answer to such divisiveness is the believer's submission to God.

THE TRUTH ABOUT CONFLICTS (4:1–5)

Their Source (v. 1)

James's readers apparently were plagued by conflicts and disputes. He addressed these conflicts directly. In effect, his opening in verse 1 was a question to ask his readers whether they wanted to submit to the will of God or satisfy their own desires for the pleasures of this world. The two choices before them were (1) friendship with the world, or (2) friendship with God.

James identified the source of their conflicts as "cravings." The point of verse 1 is that evil desires are within every human being, and they must be confronted.

Their Outcome (vv. 2–3)

James moved on to describe the outcome of unchecked evil desire in a person's life. He returned to his theme of 1:14–15, where he wrote of the deadly effects of evil desire in a person's life: "One is tempted by one's own desire, being lured and enticed by it; then, when the desire has conceived, it gives birth to sin, and that sin, when it is fully grown, gives birth to death" (NRSV).

Want

This word is a compound word in the Greek text. It is made up of the preposition "upon" and the verb "to desire." It means "to desire something earnestly," emphasizing the inward impulse rather than the object desired (*Vine's Complete Expository Dictionary of Old and New Testament Words* [Nashville: Thomas Nelson, 1996], 162).

James identified their "cravings" in two different ways: "You want something but don't get it" and "you kill and covet, but you cannot have." These two cravings likely parallel the twin evils of chapter 3—bitter envy and selfish ambition.

Wanting What They Do Not Have. At the root of the conflict James wrote about *desire.* Throughout the New Testament, its writers warn that the desires for the things of this world are always a threat to the spiritual life of the believer.

Coveting What They Cannot Obtain. Coveting is the willingness to steal what belongs to someone else. Such desire becomes idolatry.

The result of the ruthlessness in the hearts of these believers is quarreling and fighting, which has the potential to lead to murder. (See the words of Jesus in Matt. 15:19.) Although some interpreters take James's reference to murder as a metaphor, the connection between the frustration of not having and envying with the act of murder is certainly a reality in today's world.

James closed this section with a reference to prayer that is consistent with true faith. These quarrelers did not rely on God for provision, but rather were driven to fight for what they wanted. When they did ask of God, they did so with the wrong motives.

"You do not have, because you do not ask God" (v. 2). Rather than asking God for wisdom (James 1:5), they relied on wisdom that comes from the world. Had they asked God, they would have found wisdom and peace as the outcome.

"*You do not receive, because you ask with wrong motives*" (v. 3). These believers failed to receive because they asked wrongly. Their motives were shaped, not by God's wisdom, but by their own evil desires. Those motives were rooted in their own "pleasures." James wrote that they intended to "spend" what God gives them on their pleasures. The word *spend* refers to the act of securing enjoyment. It is the same word Jesus used in His parable of the prodigal son in describing the lost son's squandering of his wealth in "wild living" (Luke 15:13–15). Their goal was to exchange, or cash in, for whatever gain they could make from God's gifts.

James's observation on the prayer life of these individuals revealed that they were impatient people bent on exercising their own will over God's. They were not interested in being guided by God's Word or His will. True prayer is not self-centered, but an act of humility before God.

The Enmity of Friendship with the World (vv. 4–5)

James addressed his readers harshly as "adulterers!" This term is an Old Testament simile for unfaithfulness. His mention of it likely brought to his readers' minds the standard Old Testament image of the covenant relationship between God and His people (Isa. 54:4–8). In that passage, Israel is the wife of the Lord (Jer. 31:21; Hos. 3:1; Ezek. 23:45). By making this correlation, James implied that his readers were having an "affair" with the world.

James labeled this condition as "friendship with the world" (v. 4). This indicates their hatred toward God. A person cannot be friends with the world and love God at the same time. In this

Psalm 34:14–17 reinforces James's teaching in this passage: "Turn from evil and do good; seek peace and purse it. The eyes of the LORD are on the righteous and his ears are attentive to their cry; the face of the LORD is against those who do evil.... The righteous cry out, and the LORD hears them."

Hatred

The word translated "hatred" by the NIV is literally the word *enmity*. It is a word that indicates active hostility toward God. In this passage, it is intended to be the opposite of friendship.

way, spiritual adultery is synonymous with being an enemy of God.

Warnings Against Believers Flirting with the World

PASSAGE	WRITER	WARNING
Matt. 6:24	Matthew, quoting Jesus	"No one can serve two masters. Either he will hate the one and love the other, or he will be devoted to the one and despise the other. You cannot serve both God and Money."
2 Tim. 3:2, 4	Paul, writing to Timothy	"People will be . . . lovers of pleasure rather than lovers of God."
1 John 2:15	John, writing to believers	"Do not love the world or anything in the world. If anyone loves the world, the love of the Father is not in him."

Scholars have found verse 5 difficult to translate, as there are a variety of ways the verse can be punctuated, leading to different translations.

Here are some of the possible interpretations:

1. James is asking if the spirit which God has put in us longs to the point of envying (ASV).
2. God's Spirit which He placed in us yearns with jealousy over us (Weymouth).
3. God yearns jealously over the Spirit which He has placed within us.

N

- Because James's readers were plagued by
- conflicts and disputes, he asked them
- whether they wanted to submit to the will of
- God or to satisfy their own desires for the
- pleasures of this world. The two choices
- before them were friendship with the world
- or friendship with God. Friendship with the
- world is spiritual adultery, making them
- enemies of God.

BEING A FRIEND OF GOD (4:6–10)

Grace for the Humble (v. 6)

James provided the antidote to spiritual adultery by quoting from the Old Testament book of Proverbs: "He [God] mocks proud mockers but gives grace to the humble" (Prov. 3:34). In addition to this Old Testament quotation, James reminded his readers that God gives "more" grace, and that by appropriating that grace, they could overcome their spiritual sins. Paul's words, "where sin increased, grace increased all the more" (Rom. 5:20), would certainly support James's text. A key point to be gained from this verse is that unlike some of James's readers, whose envy was directed toward all, God maintains a favorable disposition toward believing sinners.

Exercising for Humility (vv. 7–10)

Building on the foundation he laid in verse 6, James began a series of imperatives that span the next four verses. These commands, in effect, are his recipe for humility or a how-to on repentance. James provided his readers with these progressive steps of spiritual self-discipline, each being a means of entering into an intimate relationship with God.

Proud

Our English translation of the word *proud* is an interesting word in James's Greek text. It is a compound word made up of the preposition "above" or "beyond" and the basic word "proud." The prefixed preposition heightens the word's basic meaning. This word refers to a person who is *haughty* or *arrogant*, a person who thinks above and beyond that which is proper. "Like our vernacular 'stuck-up folks'" (A. T. Robertson, *Word Pictures in the New Testament*, vol. 6, "General Epistles and Revelation of John," 52).

Submit Yourselves to God (v. 7). To "submit" was a military term, meaning literally to be "arranged or ordered under." To submit is to align oneself under the authority of another. All conflict resolution needs to start with a renewed submission to God by the internal act of submission to His authority.

Resist

The word *resist* is a compound word in the Greek text, made up of the prefixed preposition "against" and the verb "to cause to stand." It carries the ideas of withstanding and opposing and is rendered "resist." A modern-day application of this Greek word (*anthistemi*) relates to medicine. A person suffering from an allergy might take an *antihistamine* to block histamines and reduce, or resist, the effects of allergens.

Resist the Devil (v. 7). James next instructed his readers to put up an active resistance to the devil and the influence he wields in their lives. James did not advocate an offensive approach toward the devil, but rather a defensive posture.

Resistance is an effective attack for the believer. The result is that the devil will flee. This picture brings to mind Luke 4:13: "When the devil had finished all this tempting, he left him until an opportune time." When met with Jesus' resistance toward his temptation, Satan's course of action was to leave. It is important to note that Jesus used Scripture in His resistance to the devil's wiles. The believer will do well to take the Lord's example to heart.

Come Near to God (v. 8). This step begins with a positive exhortation and concludes with a promise. Nearness to God is a basic call of the Christian faith. It is an act of contrition, and it involves letting go of and rejecting all evil practices and false teachings. The promise to James's readers was that if they took this step, God would draw near to them.

Wash Your Hands and Purify Your Hearts (v. 8). These are reconciling actions that bring to mind the ritual purity required of worshipers and priests at the Temple. The second prophetic call is to the purification of the heart. Drawing near to God involves a commitment of the will to cleanse one's hands to assume a submissive spirit so that one may purify the heart. By washing the hands and purifying the heart, the believer is turning from sin and double-mindedness.

James intentionally combined the hand and the heart, as they both must move in harmony in action and commitment before God. A morality rooted in sincere faith requires an inner life that is purified and which corresponds with the character of God (cp. Matt. 5:8; 1 Tim. 1:5). As the believer draws near to God, God and the heart of the believer come together, and one should mirror the other. Noted Bible teacher Warren Wiersbe states that the concept of drawing near to God is more a case of "nearness is likeness." It is an observation that James's teaching here would seem to validate.

Grieve, Mourn, and Wail; Change Your Laughter to Mourning and Your Joy to Gloom (v. 9). These four imperatives, or commands, call for a deep transformation of a person's attitude toward God. James presented a progression that the believer is to use for attacking his or her own heart and bringing it into submission to God.

Grieve. This word means to undergo hardship. It refers to dealing with one's inner attitude of repentance.

Mourn. This action is self-contained and is the expression of one's grief.

Wail. The grief that James described here is more than a heartache; it's a heavy grief that brings tears to the eyes. Certainly, the removal of deeply rooted sin would result in such a release.

Change Laughter to Mourning. This refers to the act of turning from the laughter of an arrogant, autonomous fool to true humility before God.

Matthew 23:12 provides insight into the meaning of this promise: "Whoever exalts himself will be humbled, and whoever humbles himself will be exalted."

Humble Yourselves Before the Lord (v. 10). This is a command to the believer to humble himself or herself before God. This humility is to be a matter of the believer's relating wholeheartedly to God in recognition of God's total claim upon the believer's life. To this command James attached the promise, "He will lift you up."

James's Recipe for Humility

COMMAND	VERSE	THE BELIEVER'S PROPER RESPONSE
Submit yourselves	v. 7	The believer is to submit to the authority of God.
Resist the devil	v. 7	The believer is to put up an active resistance to the devil and the influence he wields.
Come near to God	v. 8	The believer must reject all evil practices and false teachings and approach God with a submissive spirit.
Wash your hands and purify your hearts	v. 8	The believer needs to make a commitment to purify the heart and turn from sin and double-mindedness.
Grieve, mourn, and wail	v. 9	The believer is to attack his or her own heart and bring it into submission to God.
Change your laughter to mourning and your joy to gloom	v. 9	The believer needs to turn from an attitude of arrogance to true humility before God.
Humble yourselves before the Lord	v. 10	The believer needs to relate wholeheartedly to God in recognition of God's total claim upon his or her life.

■ *James provided the antidote to spiritual adul-*
■ *tery by quoting from the Old Testament book of*
■ *Proverbs: "He mocks proud mockers but gives*
■ *grace to the humble" (Prov. 3:34). Then He*
■ *provided His recipe for humility—a progres-*
■ *sion of steps, each being a means of entering*
■ *into a more intimate relationship with God.*

Warning Against Slander (4:11)

James opened this section by addressing his readers as "brothers" rather than "adulterous people." He began his teaching by issuing the command to "not slander one another." (He used the verb for "slander" three times; it is translated "slander" once and "speak against" twice.) "Slander was considered a vice in the ancient world, and by interjecting it here, James pronounced a judgment on their behavior that perhaps they were not expecting" (Kurt A. Richardson, *James,* The New American Commentary, vol. 36 [Nashville: Broadman & Holman, 1997], 194).

James went on to reveal more about the realities of slander.

Slander is an act of condemnation. Those who slander are really condemning the one they speak against because they are passing judgment on that person. Only God can judge, because only He knows the secrets of the heart and can judge them. Believers certainly have the right to preach the gospel, announce God's forgiveness of sins, and forgive the sins of others committed against them personally. But no person has the right to judge another person who has sinned, thereby claiming to know God's final judgment about a person.

Slander

The word for "slander" is a compound word made up of two words: a prefixed preposition meaning "against" and the verb "to speak." Literally, the word means "to speak against," "to defame," "to speak evil of." The word is applied to scenarios where harsh words are spoken about a person who is not present.

Slander judges God's law. When believers engage in judging others, they slander the law of God. Believers are to accept the law. They are not to place themselves in a position of rival judgment with God's. This law requires them to exercise mercy toward others, since they themselves have received God's mercy.

GOD ALONE IS THE LAWGIVER (4:12)

His Authority (v. 12a)

The Greek text does not use the word *only*, but says "there is one lawgiver." This implies that there is only one lawgiver.

His Abilities (v. 12b)

God—the only lawgiver—is able to save and to destroy. Judgment is His alone.

He is able to save. God is the great deliverer, and only He has the ability eternally to save or rescue a person.

He is able to destroy. Likewise, only God has the ability to condemn a person.

The combination of the terms *save* and *destroy* is a picture of God's power (see Matt. 10:28). It is also a common idea in the Old Testament (Deut. 32:39; 2 Kings 5:7).

- *James emphatically issued the command to*
- *"not slander one another."*
- *Slander is an act of condemnation, and it*
- *judges God's law. Believers need to be careful*
- *not to judge others, but rather exercise mercy*
- *toward others. Only God has the ability to*
- *judge.*

WHEN BUSINESS IS A SPIRITUAL LIABILITY (4:13–17)

The Irony of Boasting (vv. 13–14)

As an example of boasting, James used the hypothetical, overconfident business dealer. He made the point that this businessman is confidently predicting the future, but without involving or considering God.

Mists in the Bible

James focused on the irony of boasting about tomorrow, reminding his readers that they know nothing about their future. He then presented a metaphor to illustrate the shortness of life: "You are a mist." Mists are transitory; they are here now and then gone! Our lives are like a morning mist that the sun soon burns away. The lesson is that human life is transitory; therefore, the believer must place his or her trust in God. Our lives are in His hands.

In the Bible, a mist often appears as a symbol for something that quickly passes away. It can refer to water, fog, or clouds. The metaphor of the mist in James 4:14 is quantitative rather than qualitative. Mists do not last long in Palestine. Their form is transitory. This evaporation is a fitting way to refer to the ephemeral attribute of human life. (Taken from the *Holman Bible Dictionary* and Kurt A. Richardson, *James*, The New American Commentary, vol. 36 [Nashville: Broadman & Holman, 1997], 199.)

The Norm of Human Activities (v. 15)

James informed his readers that there is one norm by which the life of faith is to be lived out in the temporal environment of the world— "God wills." Life is lived, but only if God wills.

The Sinfulness of Presumption (vv. 16–17)

The only rightful place boasting has in the Christian life is if it is done in reference to the work of God. But this is not the kind of boasting to which James referred in these verses. His readers were, instead, bragging arrogantly. James used two closely connected terms to describe their activities—"boasting" and "bragging."

Boast. To boast means to glory in something. Those who were boasting were doing so without any reference to God.

63

Brag. Bragging is pretension or arrogance in word and deed. It's boasting with the goal of impressing others.

Not only were these people boasting; they boasted about the fact that they boasted! They took pride in being this kind of people.

This chapter concludes with the Bible's best statement, negatively expressed, of the Christian ethic: "Therefore, to one who knows the right thing to do and does not do it, to him it is sin" (NASB).

- *Human life is transitory; it is but a morning*
- *mist that the sun quickly burns away.*
- *Because we know nothing about what tomor-*
- *row holds, it is imperative that we place our*
- *trust in God. Our lives are in His hands.*

QUESTIONS TO GUIDE YOUR STUDY

1. What is the source of conflict in the believer's life? What can be the outcome of such conflict? What is the believer's responsibility regarding conflict?
2. What did James mean by the phrase "friendship with the world"?
3. James presented a sort of "recipe" for humility. What are the steps to humility, and what must the Christian do to maintain progress toward humility?
4. What is slander? Why is it so destructive? What can a believer do to avoid slander?

JAMES 5

In this final chapter, James began by returning to the theme of the rich. He delivered strong words about the dependence upon and the abuse of wealth. Other themes include patience in the face of suffering and prayer as a central activity of the church.

JUDGMENTS AGAINST THE RICH (5:1–6)

James returned to his theme of the sins of the rich and the dangers of their wealth. (His previous treatments are 1:10–11 and 2:3–6.) Of all the New Testament passages about sins of the rich, these six verses stand out. The tremendous importance of this topic seems to have compelled James to return to it in the closing portion of his letter.

The Misery of Hoarding (vv. 1–3)

Here James expressed anger against the rich because of the way they had treated the poor and less fortunate. Immediately he addressed the future condemnation of the wicked rich: "the misery that is coming upon you." In verse 2 he presented the truth about the greed and selfish hoarding that had consumed some of the rich among his readers. He used several graphic statements to portray the degrading influence of wealth.

"Your wealth has rotted" (v. 2). In the ancient world, land and its produce were considered wealth. The picture is of the produce or crop having rotted. The verb tense James used indicates the state or condition of the wealth. This statement and the following two are prophetic in their anticipation.

"Moths have eaten your clothes" (v. 2). The clothing of the rich had been moth-eaten. James might have intended a connection between the "fine clothes" of 2:2 and the moth-eaten garments here.

"Your gold and silver are corroded" (v. 3). The precious metals of the rich were corroded and rusted. (Although gold and silver do not rust, James used his prophetic license here to make a point.) Rusted metals are no longer useful. James prophesied that the gold and silver of the rich would lose their value as investments when God's judgment comes.

These strong words echo the insights of our Lord, who warned, "Do not store up for yourselves treasures on earth, where moth and rust destroy, and where thieves break in and steal. But store up for yourselves treasures in heaven, where moth and rust do not destroy, and where thieves do not break in and steal. For where your treasure is, there your heart will be also" (Matt. 6:19–21).

With these three illustrations, James made a statement that trusting in wealth is a mistake because the idea that it retains its value is a myth. Amassing and trusting in wealth is a damaging and degrading attitude (see Matt. 13:22; Mark 4:19; Luke 8:14; 12:21; 1 Tim. 6:9). The ill-gotten wealth of these rich people was evidence of their moral depravity. James wrote: "Their corrosion will testify against you and eat your flesh like fire." In the end, corrosion destroys both the wealth and its holder.

God's Future Judgment of the Wicked Rich

RICHES	IN JUDGMENT	TRUTH ABOUT ILL-GOTTEN WEALTH
Wealth	Will be "rotted"	Hoarded wealth will be gone.
Clothing	Will be "moth-eaten"	Clothing will be destroyed.
Gold and silver	Will be "corroded"	Investment values will be lost.

The Misery of the Innocent (vv. 4–6)
James condemned the ill-gotten wealth of the rich because it had been accumulated through

fraud and at the expense of others. He issued several indictments against the rich.

Failure to pay the workmen (v. 4). Because of their greed, the rich landowners failed to pay their workers for services rendered.

The Defrauded Cry Out in Accusation (v. 4). The anguished cries of the defrauded "have reached the ears of the Lord Almighty." In ancient times, fraud was perpetrated by rich landowners against the poor day laborers. In today's complex, industrialized nations, however, fraud by the rich is perpetrated not just against manual laborers, but against consumers, taxpayers, underprivileged nations, and disorganized masses of common people without an earthly advocate. The fraud is perpetrated through fixed prices, fixed taxes, fixed tariffs, and fixed programs designed to protect the vested interests of the rich at the expense of the poor.

James told his readers that God is patient, but He is not asleep. At the right time, He will deliver His judgment.

The Luxury and Self-Indulgence of the Rich (v. 5). The callousness of the rich was rooted in their self-indulgence. They lived in luxury and self-centered pleasure at the expense of their laborers. In the ancient world, luxurious living was regarded as moral laxity. James told these wealthy ones that they were actually fattening themselves for the "slaughter."

The Murder of Innocent Men (v. 6). James declared that the rich had "condemned and murdered innocent men." He added that these men were not opposing the rich. James used a present tense of the verb "oppose" to bring the action to the attention of his readers. The

Such economic oppression was an urgent matter, as many of the laborers of the ancient world were transients, or foreigners. Sadly, the wages due them never left the vaults of the rich.

treatment of the laborers was senseless, emphasizing the depraved nature of the rich.

- *James expressed anger toward the rich*
- *because of their mistreatment of the poor and*
- *less fortunate. Immediately he addressed the*
- *future condemnation of the wicked rich. God*
- *will eventually judge the wicked rich.*

THE PRACTICE OF ENDURANCE (5:7–12)

This concluding section of James is united by the theme of the believers' exercise of faith and submission to James's teaching. The goal of his exhortations was to encourage and unite his readers as a community of Christ. It is to be a patience that endures "until the Lord's coming" (v. 7).

Patience Among Friends (vv. 7–11)

James began by encouraging his "brothers" to be patient in the midst of their suffering. He referred to trials brought about by injustices done to them.

James used three illustrations to encourage a lifestyle of persistent devotion in serving God.

1. The Farmer (v. 7). James used the illustration of a farmer who plants and then waits for the rains to produce a crop. Because many of his readers were agrarian laborers, "farm hands," this was likely a very appropriate illustration for James's original audience. Eventually, the farmer's patient endurance pays off and the land yields its valuable crop. The wise farmer learns to wait patiently for the harvest. James exhorted his readers to do the same regarding the Lord's

---

Patient

The Greek word behind our English translation "patient" is an interesting compound word. It is made up of the words "long" and "temper," and means "to be long-tempered." "The word describes the attitude which can endure delay and bear suffering and never give in" (Fritz Rienecker, *Linguistic Key to the Greek New Testament* [Grand Rapids: Zondervan, 1980], 740).

coming. In addition to patiently waiting, his readers are also to "stand firm" and not "grumble" among themselves. All three actions are involved in waiting for the Lord's coming.

Waiting for the Harvest

EXHORTATION	EXTENDED MEANING
Be patient	Patiently wait
Stand firm	Strengthen your heart
Don't grumble	Don't cultivate a spirit of grumbling

2. Old Testament Prophets (v. 10). The prophets suffered greatly because of their faithfulness and obedience to God. They displayed the proper attitude of faith in the midst of trials. They are worthy of imitation. James, in fact, invited his readers to do just that, as believers (then and now) share with the prophets the experience of suffering in patience.

3. Job (v. 11). Job is an example of patient endurance in suffering. The words of the Lord as He addressed Satan in Job 2:3 provide us with an important insight about Job.

What James showed with the illustration of Job is this great truth about trials: God allows the righteous to be tested so He may prove their faith.

"Then the Lord said to Satan, 'Have you considered my servant Job? There is no one on earth like him; he is blameless and upright, a man who fears God and shuns evil. And he still maintains his integrity, though you incited me against him to ruin him without any reason'" (Job 2:3).

Our Examples of Patience

EXAMPLE	LESSON TO BE LEARNED
The farmer	We must patiently wait for God.
The prophets	We must maintain attitudes of faithfulness and obedience.
Job	We must suffer trials to prove our faith.

James closed this section with mention that the "Lord is full of compassion and mercy" (v. 11). The significance in his focus on these attributes of God is that they are the primary attributes of God in His covenant with Israel. These character traits identify the God who blessed Job and the prophets and who will bless James's readers.

■ *The goal of this section of James's letter was*
■ *to encourage and unite his readers as a com-*
■ *munity of Christ. Their patience is to be one*
■ *that endures "until the Lord's coming" (v. 7).*
■ *Using illustrations of the farmer, the proph-*
■ *ets, and Job, James showed the character of*
■ *the kind of patience that endures life's cir-*
■ *cumstances and experiences.*

Rejection of Oaths (v. 12)

Returning to the grave concern about speech and the tongue, which he has frequently addressed in his letter, James sounded his final note on the subject. To his readers he commanded, "Do not swear." This command referred to the taking of oaths.

In times of distress, Christians could easily use God's name in a careless, irreverent way. James warned against invoking God's name to guarantee truth, calling for truthfulness so consistent that no oath was needed. "Let your 'Yes' be yes, and your 'No,' no, or you will be condemned."

EFFECTIVE PRAYER (5:13–18)

James urged his readers to pray in all circumstances, including blessing, trouble, sickness, and sin. Using the illustration of Elijah, James showed that the prayer of the righteous person is powerful and effective.

Oaths

In the Bible, symbolic acts often accompanied an oath. Invoking the name of the reigning monarch was another symbolic act joined with oath-taking. Using the Lord's name in an oath appeals directly to His involvement regarding testimony and establishes Him as the supreme enforcer and judge. To violate the Lord's name is to violate the Lord; therefore, oaths that use God's name carelessly are condemned (Exod. 20:7; Lev. 19:12).

Prayer for Times of Trouble (v. 13a)

"Is any of you in trouble?" was James's opening question to his readers regarding prayer. The kind of "trouble" he referred to is when believers suffer evil or hardship. When believers are tempted to grumble against one another, prayer serves as the antidote to grumbling. James's previous instructions on prayer tell us that this prayer should be:

* for wisdom (1:5) and
* wholehearted (1:6).

Prayer for Times of Blessing (v. 13b)

James posed a second question, "Is anyone happy?" Times of happiness are a blessing from God. The believer's proper response for these times is praise and gratitude toward God. James's implication seems to be that this praise is to be shared with the rest of the local Christian community or church.

Prayer for Times of Sickness (vv. 14–15)

In these two verses, James's teaching emphasized the community of Christian faith. Problems of sin and sickness challenge unity within a church or fellowship of believers. As with happiness, times of sickness are to be shared with other believers. In verse 14, James set forth a threefold pattern for prayer on behalf of the sick:

1. The sick person is to call the elders.
2. The elders are to anoint the sick person with oil.
3. The elders are to pray over the sick person for healing.

James told his readers that "the prayer of faith," not prayer based on the wrong motives (James 4:3), will heal the sick person. In describing God's response to their praying, James wrote that

Paul wrote in Col. 3:16: "Let the word of Christ dwell in you richly as you teach and admonish one another with all wisdom, and as you sing psalms, hymns and spiritual songs with gratitude in your hearts to God."

"Brothers, if someone is caught in a sin, you who are spiritual should restore him gently. But watch yourself, or you also may be tempted. Carry each other's burdens, and in this way you will fulfill the law of Christ" (Gal. 6:1–2).

"While Calvin, Luther and other expositors think that the practice of annointing, along with the power to heal, was meant to be confined to the apostolic age, it is doubtful that such a restriction can be maintained." Douglas J. Moo, *James,* Tyndale New Testament Commentaries (Grand Rapids: William B. Eerdmans Publishing Company, 1985), 179.

the Lord will "raise up" the sick person. It is a word used for resurrection—a restoration of life.

In Bible times, oil or ointment was used as a medicine in the treatment of wounds (Luke 10:34). James 5:14 may refer either to a symbolic use of oil or to its medicinal use. The anointing with oil is not merely a kind of home remedy. As it is applied, the name of the Lord Jesus is to be invoked. Olive oil, according to Old Testament and Jewish understanding, was prized for its nurturing of human well being and for its healing properties. In Jesus' and His disciples' ministry, olive oil was used in their healings of the sick when combined with the preaching of repentance. "They went out and preached that people should repent. They drove out many demons and anointed many sick people with oil and healed them" (Mark 6:12–14). (Taken from the *Holman Bible Dictionary* and Kurt A. Richardson, *James,* The New American Commentary, vol. 36 [Nashville: Broadman & Holman, 1997], 233.)

James's next statement (v. 15*b*) raised the question about the connection between sin and sickness. Although sickness can be a consequence of sin, this is not always the case.

In John's Gospel, Jesus encountered a man who had been blind all his life. His disciples asked whether the man had sinned or his parents. Jesus answered that it was neither the man nor his parents, "but this happened so that the work of God might be displayed in his life" (John 9:3).

Earlier in John's Gospel (5:1–18), Jesus healed a man who had been crippled for thirty-eight years. Not long after Jesus healed the man, he saw him in the Temple and said, "Behold, you have become well; do not sin anymore so that nothing worse may befall you" (NASB).

Prayer for Times of Sin (v. 16)

James continued his instruction on prayer by telling his readers that their entire church or community should be characterized by mutual confession of sin. Paul's instruction for correcting a believer who has fallen into sin surely included mutual confession.

A key point here is that mutual confession leads to prayer for each other. Under the covenant with Israel, specific men were designated as priests. Under the new covenant, all believers are priests and have the privilege of interceding for their brothers and sisters in Christ—bringing them to Jesus Christ, our great High Priest.

James described the prayer of the true believer as "powerful" and "effective." Although these terms have overlapping meanings, both provide unique insight into the kind of prayer that accomplishes God's purposes.

Four friends brought a paralyzed man to Jesus. Jesus surprised and angered some of the crowd by telling the paralytic that his sins were forgiven. This was surprising because the most obvious need of the man was for physical healing. But Jesus went to the primary need first. Some of the religious leaders were angry, thinking to themselves that only God could forgive sin. Jesus perceived their thoughts and responded: "Why are you reasoning about these things in your hearts? Which is easier, to say to the paralytic, 'Your sins are forgiven'; or to say, 'Arise, and take up your pallet and walk'? But in order that you may know that the Son of Man has authority on earth to forgive sins—He said to the paralytic—'I say to you, rise, take up your pallet and go home.' And he rose and immediately took up the pallet and went out in the sight of all" (Mark 2:8–12, NASB).

The Example of Elijah (v. 17)

Powerful and effective

J. B. Phillips's paraphrase illuminates these characteristics of a righteous person's prayer: "Tremendous power is made available through a good man's earnest prayer."
The Amplified Bible says that such prayers "make tremendous power available—dynamic in its working."

James used an Old Testament example to illustrate effective prayer. Elijah prayed, and God withheld rain from the earth for three and one-half years. Then God sent rain again at Elijah's request. First Kings 17:1 records his first prayer: "Now Elijah the Tishbite . . . said to Ahab, 'As the LORD, the God of Israel, lives, whom I serve, there will be neither dew nor rain in the next few years except at my word.'" His prayer to restore the rain is found in 1 Kings 18:41–42.

"Elijah was a man just like us" means that he had the same kinds of feelings as we do, endured the same kind of circumstances we face, and had the same life experiences as we do. The NRSV translates this phrase, "Elijah was a human being like us." The idea that he had our same nature "indicates that the power of Elijah's prayer did not lie in his supernatural greatness, but rather in his humanity" (Fritz Rienecker, *Linguistic Key to the Greek New Testament* [Grand Rapids: Zondervan, 1980], 742).

Elijah's example illustrates everything that James wrote about a faith that rejects worldly standards of judgment in favor of divine standards. An important point of this illustration is that Elijah knew the will of God concerning the signs of drought and rain. This knowledge was why he prayed so fervently. By applying the Word of God, all believers can know God's will and then do His will through their own fervent praying. James's statement "If it is the Lord's will" (4:15) comes to mind. This fervent praying is appropriate for all seasons and circumstances of life.

Prayer for Every Season

SEASON OF LIFE	NATURE OF THE BELIEVER'S PRAYER
In times of trouble	For strength to endure
In times of blessing	A song of praise
In times of sickness	A request for healing
In times of sin	Intercession

- *James urged his readers to pray in all circumstances, including times of blessing, trouble, sickness, and sin. Using the illustration of Elijah, James showed that the prayer of the righteous person is powerful and effective.*

THE MINISTRY OF RESTORATION (5:19–20)

The disciplined Christian life involves not only patience and purity of speech and prayer but also persistence in rescuing the perishing. At the very heart of the life and work of the church is restoration of the fallen, the finding of the lost, and the saving of sinners. Again, in this passage James used the only word for sin that he employed in his writing, and that is the word that means "to miss the mark." It is the nature of human beings to stray from God's way, to miss the moral targets that He has established, and to turn from the ideals that God has ordained.

Restoration takes place in view of:

1. God's mercy, which James tells us triumphs over judgment (2:13).
2. God's requirement that believers humble themselves (4:6–10).

To anyone willing, the way "back" to God and to life is to turn "from the error of his way" to save one's soul from "death and cover over a multitude of sins" (v. 20). Morally stumbling men and women who are missing God's mark of their lives, who are sick unto death, can find grace and the good life when they trust and obey Him.

Turns

This word is a compound word made up of the prefixed preposition "towards" and the verb "to turn." It literally means "to turn about" or "to turn toward" something. It is often translated "convert" because it describes a person's turning around or about. Associated with this turning around is repentance and faith.

■ *At the very heart of the life and work of the*
■ *church is restoration of the fallen, the finding*
■ *of the lost, and the saving of sinners. To any-*
■ *one willing, the way "back" to God and to*
■ *life is the way of turning "from the error of*
■ *his way" to save one's soul from "death and*
■ *cover over a multitude of sins" (v. 20).*

CONCLUSION

The call of James to do the gospel has been debated, criticized, and even ignored. His call needs to be heard. There may be several keys to the lost radiance of the modern church, but one of those keys is in plain view in the gospel according to James. It is the key that unlocks the door between faith and works and once again joins that which God never meant to be separated. The joys, victories, and triumphs of pure religion are for those who live under the conviction that Jesus Christ is Lord and who are doers of the Word.

QUESTIONS TO GUIDE YOUR STUDY

1. According to James, what judgment awaits the rich who oppress the poor and hoard wealth?
2. What can we learn from James's illustrations about patience in 5:7–12?
3. What is effective prayer? What makes it so powerful in the life of the believer?
4. What is the significance of the ministry of restoration? Why is it necessary? What does it involve?

The following list is a collection of the source works used for this volume. All are from Broadman & Holman's list of published reference resources, to accommodate the reader's need for more specific information, and/or for an expanded treatment of the epistle of James. All of these works will greatly aid in the reader's study, teaching, and presentation of James. The accompanying annotations can be helpful in guiding the reader to the proper resources.

Adams, J. McKee, rev. by Joseph A. Callaway, *Biblical Backgrounds*. This work provides valuable information on the physical and geographical settings of the New Testament. Its many color maps and other features add depth and understanding.

Blair, Joe, *Introducing the New Testament*, pp. 191–95. Designed as a core textbook for New Testament survey courses, this volume helps the reader in understanding the content and principles of the New Testament. Its features include special maps and photos, outlines, and discussion questions.

Cate, Robert L., *A History of the New Testament and Its Times*. An excellent and thorough survey of the birth and growth of the Christian faith in the first-century world.

Holman Bible Dictionary. An exhaustive, alphabetically arranged resource of Bible-related subjects. An excellent tool of definitions and other information on the people, places, things, and events of the Bible.

Holman Bible Handbook, pp. 757–61. A comprehensive treatment that offers outlines, commentary on key themes and sections, and full-color photos, illustrations, charts, and maps. Provides an accent on the broader theological teachings of the Bible.

Lea, Thomas D., *The New Testament: Its Background and Message*, pp. 519–31. An excellent resource for background material—political, cultural, historical, and religious. Provides background information in broad strokes on specific books, including the Gospels.

Richardson, Kurt A., *James* (The New American Commentary), vol. 36. A more scholarly treatment of the text of James that provides emphases on the text itself, background, and theological considerations.

Robertson, A. T., *A Grammar of the Greek New Testament in the Light of Historical Research*. An exhaustive, scholarly work on the underlying language of the New Testament. Provides advanced insights into the grammatical, syntactical, and lexical aspects of the New Testament.

Robertson, A. T., *Word Pictures in the New Testament*, vol. 6, "The General Epistles and The Revelation of John," pp. 1–68. This six-volume series provides insights into the Greek language of the New Testament. It provides word studies as well as grammatical and background insights into the epistles of Paul.

Valentine, Foy, *Hebrews, James, 1 & 2 Peter* (Layman's Bible Book Commentary, vol. 23), pp. 43–49. A popular-level treatment of the book of James. This easy-to-use volume provides a relevant and practical perspective for the reader.

SHEPHERD'S NOTES

SHEPHERD'S NOTES

SHEPHERD'S NOTES

SHEPHERD'S NOTES